FUE 29M

Classic Cars

This edition published by Parragon in 2010

Parragon
Queen Street House
4 Queen Street
Bath BA1 1HE, UK

ISBN 978-1-4454-0833-0

Printed in China

Designed, produced and packaged by Stonecastle Graphics Limited

Text by Andrew Noakes
Designed by Paul Turner and Sue Pressley
Edited by Andrew Charman

Photographic credits:
Barry Turner, Puffin Digital: page 44.
Andrew Noakes/BMW Group PressClub: page 46 (below).
DaimlerChrysler: page 69.
GM Media: page 76.
Andrew Noakes/Ford Motor Company Archives: page 88 (below).
Giles Chapman Library: pages 89, 119, 162.
Andrew Noakes/Wieck/GM Media: page 105.
brt PHOTO/Alamy: page 108 (below).
vario images GmbH & Co.KG/Alamy: page 133 (above).
Transtock Inc./Alamy: page 159 (top).
All other photographs © LAT Photographic Digital Archive.

Front cover:1948 Talbot-Lago Type 26 Grand Sport©Car Culture/Corbis
Back cover (from left to right): Duesenberg J/SJ;Austin-Healey 100; Ford Mustang; Aston Martin DB7.
All Photographs© LAT Photographic Digital Archive.

Classic Cars

THE WORLD'S GREATEST AUTOMOBILES

Andrew Noakes

Parragon

Bath · New York · Singapore · Hong Kong · Cologne · Delhi · Melbourne

Contents

WLK 348G

Introduction

Old cars have soul and character that very few modern machines can match. Modern cars are very safe, very reliable, extremely fuel-efficient. They are often faster, invariably emit fewer pollutants and need infrequent servicing. Yet few of them offer the involvement and excitement of a classic, and none of them have the years of history that makes an old car special.

There are almost as many definitions of classic as there are classic car enthusiasts. The Classic Car Club of America has a very rigid definition, limited to 'fine or unusual' cars built between 1925 and 1948. So an Auburn Speedster is a classic, but a Model A Ford isn't. Nor are such incredible machines as the Mercedes-Benz 300 SL, Bentley Continental, Porsche 911 or Maserati Bora – all of which, by that standard, are too young to qualify. But most enthusiasts take a more pragmatic and wide-ranging view, admitting to the ranks of classics all sorts of vehicles from the early days of motoring right up to modern machinery.

Inevitably plenty of them are the rapid and sensational sports cars of each era – cars like Jaguar's XK120, E-type and XKR, Ferrari's Daytona and 246 GT, Lamborghini's Miura and Countach, and from America the Chevrolet Corvette and a whole host of V8-engined 'muscle cars' from the '60s. There are more affordable sports cars too, from the golden age of the British roadster – kicked off by cars such as the MG T-series and perpetuated by Triumph's TRs, Austin-Healey's four cylinder and six-cylinder machines and the mass-market MGB, MG Midget, Austin-

Above: *By some of the more strict definitions, the magnificent 'gullwing' Mercedes-Benz 300 SL does not qualify as a classic – but most enthusiasts would agree the term fits very well.*

Below: *The Auburn 851 Speedster is a classic in the eyes of the Classic Car Club of America, which recognises only the best cars from 1925 to 1948.*

Healey Sprite and Triumph Spitfire. Above them in the pecking order lie more sophisticated machinery from the likes of Lotus (with the Elite and Elan, and later the Elise) and Porsche (with the 356, 911 and Boxster), and from Italy the characterful sporting cars of Fiat, Alfa Romeo and Lancia.

But classic cars aren't all sports cars, or even the sports saloons which became popular from the 1960s onwards thanks to cars such as the Mini Cooper, Lotus Cortina, BMW 02 series and later the Sierra Cosworth. The classic ranks also include elegant coupés and cabriolets such as the Mercedes Benz 300 SE of the 1960s, and plush prestige saloons such as Lincoln's 1961 Continental, the Mercedes 600 or the Rolls-Royce Silver Shadow – and many more.

More humble cars make the grade too, particularly those that have mobilised the millions thanks to clever design. Henry Ford's Model T and Model A appear in these pages, and so do Herbert Austin's Seven, Ferdinand Porsche's Volkswagen and Alec Issigonis' Mini, classics all of them. And we've even mentioned a handful of cars which are interesting and historically significant despite – or in some cases because – they were flawed or unsuccessful, cars such as the Edsel, the NSU Ro80, the Chevrolet Corvair and the Daimler Dart.

Whether you are personally motivated by the thinly disguised racing cars on the road that have grabbed plaudits and headlines down the years, or perhaps the luxury saloons that offer the highest quality of engineering and design, or even the everyday machines which wrought sweeping changes to our society and our quality of life, you will find a classic car to excite you. And you will probably find it in the pages that follow.

Above: *Long-running popularity, engineering integrity and a remarkable competition career make Porsche's 911 a genuine classic.*

Below: *Speed and style at their peak: to many the Jaguar E-type is the ultimate classic car.*

Chapter 1

Pre-War Classics

Mercedes 35hp-60hp

It was Emil Jellinek, a businessman living in the south of France at the start of the 20th century, who gave the name 'Mercedes' to the products of the German Daimler car company. The first Mercedes cars were the 28hp Daimler Phoenix models he entered in a hillclimb competition in Nice in 1900. The next Mercedes models were perhaps the most significant cars of their era.

Jellinek asked Daimler to produce a faster, lighter and better-handling machine which would be more competitive in sporting events. The response from Daimler's chief engineer, Wilhelm Maybach, was a car which set a pattern for performance cars which still has echoes today.

Maybach built a new 35hp engine with, for the first time, an aluminium crankcase to reduce weight. Conventionally intake valves had been 'automatic', sucked open by vacuum in the cylinders, but Maybach arranged positive operation by a camshaft to improve valve timing. With twin carburettors – one for each pair of cylinders – the 35hp engine offered sparkling performance together with unmatched smoothness. The chassis was equally innovative: for the first time, the side members were stamped from sheet steel to save weight.

The first 35hp was test-driven at the end of November 1900, and delivered to Jellinek that December. Early in 1901 it proved its worth at the Nice speed trials, and 'Mercedes' quickly became a household name. That autumn work began on an even quicker car, the 40hp 'Simplex', and by 1903 Mercedes had introduced the 60hp, good for a then-astonishing 60mph (96.6km/h).

Above: *Wilhelm Maybach's Mercedes 60, a development of the 35hp car of 1900, set the basic layout which most performance cars would follow for decades to come.*

Below: *Innovations on the Mercedes included an alloy-block engine with positive exhaust valve operation, and a chassis made from pressed steel members.*

Rolls-Royce Silver Ghost

The car which earned Rolls-Royce the soubriquet 'the best car in the world' was the 40/50hp – more commonly known as the Silver Ghost. For nearly two decades, the Silver Ghost was for many people the ultimate in motoring luxury. Launched at London's Olympia motor show in November 1906, the Silver Ghost was lavishly engineered, neatly detailed and exquisitely manufactured. It provided an almost unmatched blend of comfort, smoothness and performance.

The key to the Silver Ghost's ability was its engine, an in-line six-cylinder unit with the cylinders cast as two blocks of three. Unusually for the time the crankshaft had a full complement of seven bearings, further aiding smoothness and reliability. The bore and stroke were both 4.5in (114mm) resulting in a capacity of 7036cc and an output of 48bhp, with vast reserves of torque available at very low engine speeds. In 1907 that flexibility was demonstrated by Rolls-Royce managing director Claude Johnson driving from Bexhill to Glasgow using only third and fourth gears, in the silver 40/50hp which was the first to be called 'Silver Ghost'. The same car proved its quality time and again in long-distance reliability runs.

More than 6000 40/50hp models were built before Rolls-Royce moved on to other models in 1925. The original Silver Ghost, Johnson's 40/50hp, was sold by Rolls-Royce in 1908 but bought back 40 years later and today it is still owned by the company. It is unlikely ever to be sold again, but must be one of the most valuable cars in the world.

Above left: *The imposing face of the 40/50hp Rolls-Royce, with the famous 'Spirit of Ecstacy' mascot atop the radiator grille.*

Above: *Exquisite workmanship and endless attention to detail were hallmarks of Rolls-Royce – this is the model that earned the title 'best car in the world'.*

Below: *Rolls-Royce built more than 6000 of the 40/50 model – better known as the Silver Ghost – between 1906 and 1925.*

Ford Model T

Henry Ford built his first car in 1896 and went into production with the two-cylinder Model A in 1903. Four- and six-cylinder cars followed over the next few years, but it was the Model T launched in 1908 that really put the Ford Motor Company on the map.

Ford designed every aspect of the 'Tin Lizzie' for cheap and easy mass production, ease of use and ease of repair. In its basic layout it was very much a conventional machine, with a simple ladder chassis and separate body and an in-line four cylinder engine mounted at the front with its gearbox behind, driving the rear wheels through a propshaft and live rear axle. It was the detailing which made it clever.

The engine was a simple 2.9-litre unit with a cast iron block and cylinder head, side valves and a three-bearing crankshaft with crude splash lubrication. Maximum power was just 20bhp, but the engine developed plenty of low-speed torque. The engine was controlled not by an accelerator pedal but by throttle and ignition timing levers mounted on the steering wheel.

The gearbox was unconventional, and made the Model T much easier to drive than many rivals. Instead of a normal manual gearbox and pedal-operated clutch, Ford employed an epicyclic geartrain which offered two forward speeds, plus reverse and neutral. High and low gears were selected using the left-hand pedal, while the middle pedal selected reverse. The right-hand pedal operated a transmission brake.

Above: *Ford knew most motorists drove on farm tracks or open country, so he fitted the Model T with transverse leaf springs to give excellent ground clearance.*

Below: *Model Ts were available with numerous different styles of bodywork, from chic two-seaters to taxicabs and trucks. This four-seater dates from 1915.*

Above: *Model Ts were fitted with a novel transmission operated by pedals – the throttle was a lever on the steering wheel.*

Ford realised that few American motorists had good roads to drive on: most had to contend with unmetalled farm tracks or open prairie. The Model T's suspension was designed with those conditions in mind. Both axles were mounted on transverse leaf springs, inverted so the centre of the spring was mounted on the chassis and the ends picked up on the axle. Though this resulted in a rather tip-toe appearance it gave the Model T excellent ground clearance to cope with the worst roads.

Ford sold 10,000 Model Ts in 1909, the first year of sales. As production quickened and the build process was further streamlined and mechanised, costs came down and Ford cut the price again and again – the tourer which had cost $850 in 1909 was just $360 by 1916, and in the same period Ford doubled his workers' wages and shortened their working day.

Production peaked at over 2 million in 1923, but by then the Model T was showing its age. More than 15 million Model T Fords were built in a production run which continued for 20 years, finally coming to an end in 1927. It made mass-production a reality, mobilised America, and expanded Ford's reach overseas. Crude though some of its engineering might be, the Model T is unquestionably one of the greatest cars of its era.

Ford Model T

Engine 2878cc in-line four

Bore x stroke 95 x 101.5mm

Valvegear Sidevalve

Fuel system Holley carburettor

Power 20bhp at 1800rpm

Suspension Front: beam axle and transverse leaf spring; rear: live axle and transverse leaf spring

Wheels Wooden-spoke

Brakes Mechanical brakes on rear wheels only

Top speed 42mph (67.6km/h)

Bentley 3-litre/4.5-litre/ Speed Six/8-litre

The magnificent machines created by W.O. Bentley are among the most recognisable of all vintage cars. Massive, powerful and fast, they are among the ultimate machines of their era.

The 3-litre arrived in 1921. It was based on a stout conventional ladder chassis frame with huge side members, on which sat an unstressed body fronted by a characteristic rounded radiator. Under the bonnet was a four-cylinder fixed-head engine with a single overhead camshaft which was shaft-driven from the front of the crankshaft and operated 16 valves.

The 3-litre developed an impressive 80bhp, while the 4½-litre which followed gave 105bhp. Even more was on tap from the famous 'blower' 4½ and six-cylinder, 6½ litre Speed Six from 1929.

Ettore Bugatti is said to have described Bentleys as 'the world's fastest lorries'. W.O. Bentley built his cars to be strong, powerful and fast, and their record in competition shows that the strategy was a success: Bentley's cars beat the French in their own Le Mans 24-hour race four times in succession, from 1927 to 1930. But Bentley's sporting success was not matched in the marketplace: the Depression arrived just as the firm went into the super-luxury arena with its 8-litre model. Bentley went into receivership in 1930 and was taken over by Rolls-Royce.

Above: *Bentley's first car was the four-cylinder 3-litre, unveiled in 1921. The 16-valve engine developed 80bhp.*

Below: *The 8-litre Bentley was built to take on Rolls-Royce, but arrived as the Depression started.*

Vauxhall 30/98

Laurence Pomeroy was a gifted engineer, but even his expertise was stretched by a request for a new competition car in March 1913. It was to be ready for the Shelsley Walsh hillclimb, just 13 weeks away…

Pomeroy's response was based on the existing 'Prince Henry' Vauxhall. A new, lightweight aluminium body and a modified 4.5-litre engine improved the car's performance to the point where it sliced eight seconds from the Shelsley record. Despite its potential the car could not go into production – war intervened, during which Vauxhall built 2000 D-type tourers as army staff cars. In 1919 the new car, designated the E-type or '30/98' was launched with a price tag of £1600, which put it firmly into the luxury bracket alongside such cars as the 3-litre Bentley. It was sold as 'The Car of Grace that sets the Pace.'

It proved to be a successful competition car, despite lacking front-wheel brakes until 1926. By then the need for better braking was all the greater thanks to a more powerful engine with overhead valve operation, and up to 120bhp.

The American giant General Motors bought Vauxhall in 1925. The OE-type 30/98 soldiered on until 1927, but it was never directly replaced – and it was many years before Vauxhall would produce another car even remotely as exciting.

Above and below: *Vauxhall's 30/98 was one of the greatest sporting cars of its era, and a serious rival for some of W.O. Bentley's more famous machines.*

Austin Seven

Herbert Austin designed the original Seven himself – according to legend, on the billiard table at his home. Everything about it was designed to be as small, light and cheap to make as possible. The chassis was made from two channel-section steel members which met at the front of the car, where they carried a transverse leaf spring suspending the front axle. At the other end each chassis rail carried a quarter-elliptic leaf spring on which the rear axle was mounted. The tiny, 696cc side-valve engine had just two bearings and 'spit and hope' lubrication without proper pressure feed. A simple doped-fabric body completed the specification.

Crude though it undoubtedly was, the Seven was the right car for the times. It reinvigorated Austin sales at a time when the company was under pressure from the rising might of Morris Motors, and it was the car which truly brought motoring to the masses in the United Kingdom – in the same way as the Model T Ford did for two decades in the US.

As a result most Sevens were simple open tourers or cramped four-seater saloons, but the two-seat Nippy and Speedy sports versions were the very cheapest sporting machines of their day – and William Lyons' Swallow company could provide stylish bodywork for the Seven at reasonable cost. By contrast Austin's racing exploits included specialised racing Sevens which were practically miniature Grand Prix cars, built with Swiss-watch precision.

Above: *The diminutive Seven was Herbert Austin's own project. It was small, light and cheap to build – and it arrived at just the right time.*

Below: *Standard bodies for Sevens included open tourers, sporting roadsters and upright saloons – and William Lyons' Swallow company provided stylish alternatives.*

Bugatti Type 41 'Royale'

Above: Vast and magnificent, the Royale is one of Bugatti's best-known cars – yet in commercial terms it was a failure. Everything about the Royale is built on a massive scale, from the 24-inch alloy wheels to the 12.8-litre engine.

Despite the 'Royale' soubriquet, Ettore Bugatti's magnificently decadent Type 41s never found a customer among the European royalty for which they were originally designed. Instead just six of these enormous, 12.8-litre machines were built, three of them remaining inside the Bugatti family and the other three being sold to private owners.

The limited production run was certainly not a reflection on the quality of the car. Like all Bugattis it was immaculately well built, and blended style with clever engineering. Brake drums were cast integrally with the massive 24-inch alloy wheels, for instance, and the vast engine had three valves for each of its eight cylinders, all driven by a single overhead camshaft.

The Type 41's problem was its huge cost – more than twice the price of a Rolls-Royce – and the nose-dive in the world economy at the end of the 1920s. It was launched at just the wrong time.

Though the Royale was ultimately a commercial failure, its engine formed the heart of a high-performance railcar designed by Bugatti in 1931 and used on French railways in the 1930s. More than 100 railcar units were built, helping Bugatti to weather the economic downturn.

The super-rare Royale is, inevitably, one of the most valuable cars in the world. One example sold at auction in 1987 for $8.7million, by some margin the highest auction price ever recorded for a car.

1930 Bugatti Type 41 'Royale'
Engine 12,763cc in-line eight
Bore x stroke 125 x 130mm
Valvegear Single overhead camshaft
Fuel system Single carburettor
Power 300bhp at 2000rpm
Suspension Front: beam axle with semi-elliptic leaf springs; rear: live axle with quarter-elliptic springs
Wheels 24in alloy wheels
Brakes Drum brakes all round
Top speed 125mph (201km/h)

Lancia Lambda

Fiat moved into the motor car business by taking control of Ceirano, a small car and bicycle workshop in Turin, Italy. One of its engineers was an eighteen-year-old named Vincenzo Lancia, who became chief tester and works racing driver. In 1906 Lancia established a company of his own, taking a Fiat colleague, Claudio Fogolin, with him.

Despite a disastrous start – Lancia's factory and all its contents were destroyed by fire – Lancia was soon well advanced with his first car, a lightweight machine with a 2.5-litre four-cylinder engine. It was called the Alpha, beginning a tradition of naming Lancia cars after Greek letters which endures to this day. Gradually the cars became more innovative, and the Lambda was the most radical of all.

It was launched in 1922, at a time when most cars had in-line engines, crude ladder chassis with separate, unstressed bodywork, and beam-axle front suspension. The Lambda was innovative in each area. Its structure was a monocoque made from pressed steel panels riveted together. At the front sat a narrow-angle V4 engine with a light-alloy block and a single cast-iron head covering both cylinder banks. It developed 50bhp from 2120cc. A novel sliding-pillar design of independent front suspension was employed, and the Lambda soon won a reputation for remarkable handling and roadholding.

Nine distinct series of Lambdas were built in a production run which continued until 1931. A V8 Dilambda was also produced, taking the company further upmarket, but it was the original V4 car which founded Lancia's reputation for quality engineering and innovation.

Above: *Pressed steel panels were riveted together to make the Lambda's monocoque structure – but there were no obvious signs of this innovation in the sparse interior.*

Below: *The stiff monocoque structure and unusual sliding pillar front suspension helped raise the Lambda's handling and roadholding to levels which were little short of remarkable for their era.*

Bugatti Type 35

Italian engineer Ettore Bugatti started building cars under his own name in 1909, but it was the Type 35 of 1924 which really put Bugatti on the map. This vehicle is the archetypal Bugatti: light, fast and built like a Swiss watch, advanced in some areas but frustratingly old-fashioned in others. The characteristic eight-spoke alloy wheels often fitted to Type 35s were one novelty, in an era when wire-spoke wheels were the norm. The 2.0-litre straight-eight engine was also innovative, with three valves per cylinder and five ball-race main bearings allowing it to reach 6000rpm and develop 90bhp. It also produced a very distinctive sound, likened at the time to 'tearing calico'.

Despite Bugatti's opposition to superchargers, a Roots-type blower was added for the 128bhp Type 35C. There was also a cheaper and less powerful Type 35A with plain bearings. Later the engine was stroked to 2.3 litres for the unsupercharged (and very rare) 35T and the supercharged 35B. The same chassis was also made available with 1.5-litre engines in the Type 37 and Type 39.

Bugatti's Type 35 was an extraordinarily successful racing car, winning hundreds of events including five consecutive Targas Florio in Sicily and the inaugural Monaco Grand Prix in 1929. It must also rank as one of the prettiest cars of the pre-war era. It's a combination which makes the Type 35 one of the most sought-after – and most valuable – of collectors' cars.

Above and below: *Bugatti's Type 35 was a phenomenally successful racing car in the 1920s and 1930s. The eight-spoke alloy wheels are a distinctive – and innovative – Bugatti characteristic.*

Alfa Romeo 6C

Vittorio Jano's arrival at Alfa Romeo marked a revolution for the Milanese firm. Jano's first job was to lay out a new supercharged Grand Prix car, the P2. It was lighter and more streamlined than previous Alfas, and was powered by a new 2.0-litre straight-eight engine with twin overhead camshafts acting on inclined valves which fed hemispherical combustion chambers. The P2 was instantly competitive.

Its engine formed the basis of a six-cylinder, single-cam motor for a new generation of road cars, known as the 6C series, in 1925. With no supercharger and only a single carburettor the first 6C 1500 was relatively underpowered, but it was just the start of a range of cars which would become renowned for their speed and style. By 1928 a quicker twin-cam 1500 Sport was available, and that was followed by a high-compression Super Sport.

Even more performance was to follow, with the introduction of a larger 1750 engine, at first in single-cam form but later in twin-cam and high-compression guises. The latter, known as the 1750 Gran Sport, delivered 85bhp and a top speed in excess of 90mph (144.8km/h).

An eight-cylinder 8C series followed, but all were expensive cars which few could afford in the Great Depression. Eventually Alfa Romeo had to rely on government money to keep it afloat, and soon Italy was embroiled in war…

Above: *Sparse interiors were the order of the day, particularly on sporting machinery such as the Alfa Romeo.*

Below: *Vittorio Jano developed the single-cam, six-cylinder 6C road car engine from the twin-cam straight eight race engine in the P2. The 6C series began in 1924 with the 1500, and continued after the war with cars such as this 6C 2500.*

Cadillac V12/V16

Above: Ron Hickman at his Jersey home Villa Devereux with his V16 Cadillac. Hickman was the principal designer of both the Lotus Elan and Europa.

Cadillac was founded by Henry M. Leland in 1903. In 1909 it became part of the General Motors combine, and quickly assumed the role of GM's prestige brand. Cadillac introduced the first commercially successful V8 engine in 1914, and the engine continued in developed form until 1927.

That year Cadillac began work on an even larger and more impressive engine. Under the direction of Ernest Seaholm, Cadillac produced a massive, 7.4-litre V16 with a 45-degree angle between the cylinder banks and a single camshaft running along the 'V'. Though its claimed output of 165bhp was not as much as competitors with less impressive complements of cylinders, the Cadillac V16 performed with unparalleled refinement.

Though the V16 arrived just after the Wall Street crash in 1929, Cadillac sold a remarkable 2500 of them in 1930. From 1931 the V16 was joined by a V12 using the same chassis and body options and sharing many engine components, and together the V12 and V16 recorded thousands of sales for Cadillac up to 1937. Thereafter both were replaced by a cheaper, wide-angle V16 which was never as popular, selling just over 500 examples from 1937 to 1940.

American rivals Packard, Lincoln and Pierce-Arrow all entered the V12 field, as did several European makes. Cadillac's only V16 rival came from Indianapolis-based Marmon, but the car was not a commercial success.

1930 Cadillac V16
Engine 7413cc 45-degree V16
Bore x stroke 76.2 x 101.6mm
Valvegear Pushrod-operated overhead valves
Fuel system Two Cadillac carburettors
Power 165bhp at 3400rpm
Suspension Front: beam axle with semi-elliptic leaf springs; rear: live axle with semi-elliptic springs
Wheels 19in bolt-on wire wheels
Brakes Drum brakes all round
Top speed 90mph (145km/h)

Ford Model A

Above: The Model A took over from the Model T as Ford's mass-market car. This one is from 1928.

Ford clung to the Model T way beyond its natural lifespan. By the time production finally ended in 1927 it was outclassed by new rivals, and that left Ford with a major problem: the car that would replace it had to be a radical departure from what had gone before.

But it was not an innovative machine, like the Model T had been. The Model T's pedal-operated epicyclic transmission was replaced by a conventional sliding-pinion gearbox controlled by a long lever and a normal pedal-operated clutch. The Model T's archaic thermo-syphon cooling was supplanted by a proper water pump in the 3.3-litre Model A. While the Tin Lizzie had brakes only on its rear wheels, the Model A was fitted with mechanical brakes all round – the state of the art in 1927. But there was one novelty: the Model A was one of the first American cars fitted with safety glass. There was a wide variety of bodies to choose from, from two-seat roadsters to two- and four-door saloons to taxis and trucks.

Ford took the bold decision to cease production of the Model T entirely and prepare for the Model A – during the summer of 1927 Ford plants around the world stood idle as production lines were refitted and workers retrained. Production of the Model A began in October and the new model went on sale in December. More than four million Model As were made before a revised Model B was introduced in 1931: Ford's gamble paid off.

Below: Safety glass was fitted to the Model A – one of the first American cars with this innovation. More than four million Model As were built between 1927 and 1931.

Duesenberg J/SJ

Brothers Fred and August Duesenberg built successful racing cars before branching out into luxury road cars with the Duesenberg Eight in 1921. But in 1926 the company came under the control of E.L. Cord, and as if the Eight had not been extravagant enough, Cord introduced a completely new Duesenberg which was bigger, heavier and even faster.

Introduced in 1928, the Model J was powered by a 6.9-litre straight-eight engine with twin overhead camshafts and four valves per cylinder. Despite its size and weight the Model J was comfortably a 100mph (161km/h) car, and customers looking for the last word in performance were catered for in 1932 with the introduction of an even more rapid supercharged SJ model. The Duesenbergs were favourites of America's rich and famous, including Clark Gable, Gary Cooper and Howard Hughes.

Though the J and SJ survived the Great Depression and continued to be built in small numbers during the early 1930s, the Auburn-Cord-Duesenberg combine as a whole struggled to make money. The collapse of the company in 1937 ended Duesenberg production, when fewer than five hundred of these amazing machines had been built. Today the size, the engineering and the glamour of these cars, together with their rarity, means that they are among the most sought-after and valuable American classics of all.

Above and below: *Sweeping lines of the Duesenberg J hint at its impressive performance – though big and heavy, this was a 100mph (161km/h) car. This one was built in 1935, just two years before the failure of the Auburn-Cord-Duesenberg combine.*

Mercedes-Benz SSK

Few cars could catch an S-type Mercedes in the 1920s. Developed by Daimler's chief engineer Ferdinand Porsche, the supercharged six-cylinder 'white elephants' gave Mercedes numerous competition victories and paved the way for Germany's domination of Grand Prix racing between the wars.

The S – for 'Sport' – models were developed from existing Mercedes, with modifications to improve performance and handling. The S-types were lower than their predecessors, with larger engines mounted further back in the chassis. The supercharger was engaged only at full throttle, delivering 180bhp from 6.8 litres. It was with an S-type Mercedes that emerging maestro Rudolf Caracciola won the first ever Nürburgring race in 1927.

The S was replaced by the 7.0-litre, 250bhp SS ('Super Sport'), from which the SSK was developed. The K stood for 'kurz', German for short, indicating that the SSK had a shorter wheelbase for crisper handling. As well as being an effective racing machine the SSK was the road-going supercar of its day, and the longer-wheelbase S-types were favourites for comfortable and extravagant touring bodies.

The ultimate derivative of the S-type was the lightweight SSKL, its chassis peppered with drillings to reduce weight to the bare minimum – about 2976lb (1350kg), some 276lb (125kg) lighter than the standard SSK. With 300bhp from its 7.1-litre straight-six engine, the SSKL could achieve an extraordinary top speed of 157mph (253km/h). Caracciola took it to victory in the Mille Miglia in 1931, the first time the race had been won by a non-Italian car and driver.

Racing regulations changed in 1934, introducing a 1653lb (750kg) maximum weight which outlawed leviathans like the SSK and instead ushered in a whole new era of racing.

1929 Mercedes-Benz SSK

Engine 7065cc in-line six

Bore x stroke 100 x 150mm

Valvegear Single overhead camshafts

Fuel system Two Mercedes-Benz carburettors, part-time Roots supercharger

Power 250bhp at 3300rpm

Suspension Front: beam axle with semi-elliptic leaf springs; rear: live axle with semi-elliptic springs

Wheels 20in wire wheels

Brakes Drum brakes all round

Top speed 117mph (188km/h)

Below: Characteristic external exhaust pipes are a feature of the short-wheelbase SSK. A lightweight SSKL version driven by Rudolf Caracciola became the first non-Italian winner of the famous Mille Miglia race in 1931.

MG Midget/Magnette

Cecil Kimber ran Morris Garages, the Oxford sales and service operation which William Morris had established alongside the Morris Motors manufacturing firm from which the huge Nuffield Organisation had sprung. Under Kimber, Morris Garages began building sporting specials based on Morris cars. Ultimately they became a separate line under the name MG.

The car which really defined MG in the minds of sporting drivers everywhere arrived in 1928. It was based on the Morris Minor, Nuffield's answer to the Austin Seven. Unlike the crude Seven, the Morris Minor had a competent ladder-type chassis and an excellent overhead-cam engine of 847cc. MG's open two-seater version, the M-type Midget, began a series of compact roadsters which would be hugely successful for MG.

Above left: *The M-type, based on the tiny Morris Minor, began a long line of successful compact sports cars for MG. Many cars were faster than the MGs, but few were more fun to drive.*

Above: *Cecil Kimber was responsible for the styling of early MGs, giving them attractive well-proportioned shapes which appealed to sporting motorists of the day.*

Left and above: *The K3 Magnette was one of MG's racing machines of the 1930s. MG was hugely successful at the banked Brooklands track, in the Ulster TT and even in sporting trials.*

Aston Martin Ulster

The first production Aston Martin appeared in 1920, but founder Lionel Martin was more interested in racing than in building cars for customers. Eventually the company ran out of money. It was rescued by the Charnwood family, who brought in an Italian-born engineer, A.C. 'Bert' Bertelli, to design a new range of cars. Bertelli penned a long chassis tourer (the T-type) and a shorter sporting car (the S-type), both launched at the London Motor Show in 1927.

Racing versions followed, and improvements designed for the racing cars were fed back to the production models. In 1928 a production sports model with a dry-sump engine was offered under the name International and in 1930 Aston Martin introduced a high-compression version called the Ulster.

But Aston Martin's finances were still shaky. When the Charnwoods departed, Bertelli struggled to keep Aston Martin afloat with the help of dealers and friends. In 1931 a 'New International' was introduced with a raft of cost-cutting measures including the use of a bought-in axle and gearbox rather than Aston's own in-house components.

After good performances at Le Mans and in the Ulster Tourist Trophy, Aston Martin introduced a new Ulster production model based on the latest Mark II chassis fitted with a narrow body and tuned engine. It also came with a guarantee that it would exceed 100mph (161km/h).

Above: *Rock drummer Nick Mason's LM18 is one of the four 1935 Aston Martin works racing cars. All four were painted 'Italian' racing red. LM18 finished 12th at Le Mans and fifth in the Ulster TT that year.*

Below: *The works cars led to an 'Ulster' production model, with a tuned engine and 100mph guarantee. But even these were not enough to ensure Aston's future success.*

Bugatti Type 57

Launched in 1934, the Type 57 Bugatti was powered by a 3.3-litre twin-cam, straight-eight engine which was derived from the unit in the 1933 Type 59 racing car. It was to prove one of the most commercially successful Bugattis, but also one of the last that the original company would build.

Stylish bodies designed by Ettore Bugatti's son Jean played a part in the Type 57's success. Jean Bugatti shaped the popular Ventoux coupé, the Stelvio cabriolet and the two-seater Atalante coupé – but the most famous of them was the Atlantic, an aerodynamic two-seater fastback. The idea had come from an experimental aerodynamic Type 57 called the Aerolithe, which was shown in 1935. The Atlantic production car of 1936 married a similar body style to a new Surbaissé (lowered) chassis, which reduced the overall height of the car by running the rear axle through the chassis members and fitting the engine with dry-sump lubrication. The ultimate specification mated the lowered chassis to a supercharged engine, in the Type 57SC.

A racing Type 59 won at Le Mans in 1939 in the hands of Pierre Veyron and Jean-Pierre Wimille. Jean Bugatti often tested Bugatti prototypes and a few weeks after the race he took the car out for a test drive, during which he lost control, hit a tree and died. He was just 30 years old.

After the war the Bugatti company would only briefly return to car manufacture with the Type 101 – which had much in common with its Type 57 predecessor.

Above and below: *Inspiration for the Bugatti Type 57 Atlantic came from an experimental aerodynamic fastback called the Aerolithe. The Atlantic's low build was aided by a dry-sump engine and special chassis.*

Chrysler Airflow

Some classics were very successful, but not all of them. The Chrysler Airflow, for all the technical innovation and ultra-modern styling which made it so advanced, was among the most heroic of failures.

The Airflow, launched in 1934, was one of the earliest examples of 'unitary' construction. There was no separate chassis, box-section load-bearing members instead being integrated into the pressed-steel body. Cost and weight can be reduced, and passenger space improved, using this type of construction. The Airflow's body was given very modern full-width styling with a smoothly curved, streamlined shape. A long-wheelbase Royal Airflow was also available.

In other respects the Airflow was conventionally engineered for its time. Three engines were available, a straight-six and straight-eights of 4.9 and 5.3 litres, driving through a live rear axle. Leaf springs were used all round, and hydraulic drum brakes were fitted at each corner.

Though streamlining was a '30s fad, the Airflow's styling failed to capture the public's imagination and it was this, as much as anything, which kept sales at low levels right up to the end in 1937. A more conventionally-styled version, the Airstream, was much more successful.

America's motor industry would be at the forefront of full-width styling when it returned with a vengeance in the 1940s, but American manufacturers would not wholeheartedly adopt unitary construction and aerodynamic shapes until the 1980s. The Airflow, combining all these innovations in the 1930s, was way ahead of its time.

1934 Chrysler Airflow
Engine 5301cc 45-degree V16
Bore x stroke 82.6 x 123.8mm
Valvegear Sidevalve
Fuel system Single carburettor
Power 115bhp at 3400rpm
Suspension Front: tubular beam axle with semi-elliptic leaf springs; rear: live axle with semi-elliptic springs
Wheels 16in steel disc wheels
Brakes Hydraulic drum brakes all round
Top speed 90mph (145km/h)

Above and below: The 1930s Chrysler Airflow was way ahead of its time, with a modern-style pressed steel monocoque body which was shaped for good aerodynamic penetration.

Citroën Traction Avant

So advanced was the Citroën Traction Avant that it survived for more than two decades from its introduction in 1934. With front-wheel drive, a monocoque chassis/body, independent front suspension and dead beam rear axle, the Traction Avant set a pattern which would not be out of place on a modern saloon car.

It was launched at the 1934 Paris show, with a choice of 1303cc or 1529cc four-cylinder engines, later joined by a 1911cc unit. With the larger engine the 'Onze Legère' (Light Eleven), as it was later known, was good for 75mph (121km/h) and offered unmatched roadholding thanks to its front-wheel drive and the low centre of gravity afforded by the unitary body.

A six-cylinder Light 15 was offered from 1938, but production of all models was interrupted by the Second World War. The production lines were restarted at the end of the war, and the Traction Avant continued well after the introduction of Citroën's advanced DS in 1955. The last one of more than 759,000 Traction Avant cars was built in July 1957.

Citroën paid a heavy price for the Traction Avant's success. Development of the car bankrupted the company, and founder André Citroën was forced to sell to his biggest creditor, the Michelin tyre company, in 1935. He died of cancer the same year, and never saw the great success of the Traction Avant.

Above and below: *The Traction Avant played every role, from family car, taxi and police car to elegant boulevard cruiser, as in this rare 'decapotable' (drophead) version.*

Auburn 851 Speedster

Auburn was a long-established wagon manufacturer which turned its attention to cars early in the 20th century. By the 1920s it was ailing, with a line-up of unexciting products, but that changed with the appointment of E.L. Cord as general manager in 1924.

Cord injected pizzazz into Auburn's products, and the company enjoyed a revival. But Auburn's fortunes proved to be a rollercoaster ride of success and disaster, and by 1934 the prospects seemed grim. What the company needed, Cord reasoned, was a high-profile model to generate interest in the brand – but little capital was available to create that model.

Stylist Gordon Buehrig came up with the answer. His Auburn Speedster cleverly incorporated some existing, though reworked, panels into a fashionable new body design. The chassis was largely carried over from previous models, but the engine that powered the Speedster was new, a supercharged straight-eight built by Lycoming and said to develop 150bhp. Famous racing driver Ab Jenkins proved the car's potential by setting a US stock car record with a 12-hour run at over 100mph (161km/h), and production Speedsters carried a plaque bearing Jenkins' signature as a result.

The Speedster helped raise Auburn's profile, but most buyers opted for more practical – and cheaper – models. Even that couldn't save Auburn, which closed in 1936. About 600 Speedsters were built, and today they are highly prized.

1935 Auburn 851 Speedster

Engine 4587cc Lycoming in-line eight

Bore x stroke 77.8 x 120.6mm

Valvegear Pushrod-operated overhead valves

Fuel system Single Stromberg carburettor plus centrifugal supercharger

Power 150bhp at 4000rpm

Suspension Front: beam axle with semi-elliptic leaf springs; rear: live axle with semi-elliptic springs

Wheels 16in bolt-on wire wheels

Brakes Drum brakes all round

Top speed 100mph (161km/h)

Below: *Existing body panels were cleverly reworked by stylist Gordon Buehrig into a far more appealing design.*

Cord 810/812

When Errett Lobban Cord took control of the Auburn Automobile Company in 1924 he injected a new dose of style and performance into the company's products. In 1929 Cord began producing cars under his own name, starting with a front-wheel drive machine, the L-29, designed by the innovative racing car engineer Harry Miller. Though technically interesting, its success was limited: the L-29 was unreliable and in any case its appearance coincided with the Wall Street crash. Production ended in 1933.

The Auburn-Cord-Duesenberg combine designed a new front-wheel drive car that year, this time to be marketed as an Auburn, but the idea was dropped. It was resurrected in 1935, this time as a Cord. The unitary-construction body of the new Cord 810, with its coffin-like engine compartment and pop-up headlamps sunk into the front wings, was instantly recognisable – but not universally admired.

Power came from a new Lycoming V8 engine, normally aspirated in the 810 and supercharged in the later 812. The engine drove forwards to a gearbox which was mounted ahead of the front wheels. The driver changed gear using a tiny lever on the steering column.

Sadly buyers were put off by high prices and the odd styling, and perhaps by memories of the untrustworthy L-29. The company's finances worsened and it finally collapsed in 1937, ending production of the 810 and 812.

Above: *The Cord's radical looks, with its 'coffin' nose and retractable headlamps in the wings, were not universally popular.*

Below: *The 'engine-turned' metal dash and art deco instrument graphics are typical touches of the 1930s.*

BMW 328

Above: The 328's driver looked out over a long, louvred bonnet under which sat a clever 'cross pushrod' engine of 2.0 litres developing 80bhp and giving sparkling performance.

Austin's tiny Seven provided the basis for the very first BMW. Known as the Dixi, it was a licence-built Seven, but from these humble beginnings, BMW quickly blossomed into a serious manufacturer and branched out with increasingly confident designs of its own. By far the best known of its pre-war products was the amazing 328 sports car.

The flowing curves of its lightweight alloy body gave the good aerodynamic performance, aided by headlamps integrated into the bodywork and a swept-back radiator grille, carrying the twin 'kidney' apertures that were now a BMW hallmark. Underneath the skin the 328 was based around the best of previous BMWs, with a tubular chassis and and straight-six engine.

The engine was improved with the addition of a new light-alloy cylinder head with efficient hemispherical combustion chambers and opposed valves. The valves were still operated by the single, low-mounted camshaft, using conventional vertical pushrods and rockers for the intake valves and a second set of short, horizontal pushrods lying across the top of the engine to operate the exhaust valves. Three downdraught Solex carburettors fed the air/fuel mixture through vertical intake ports. This sophisticated 2.0-litre engine developed 80bhp, and in racing trim delivered up to 135bhp.

Below: Flowing lines gave the 328's lightweight alloy body a stylish appearance and also gave it good aerodynamics. Note the fashionable exposed spare wheel in the tail.

Above: The twin-aperture grille was already a feature of BMWs by the time the 328 arrived.

The 328 made its public debut in Germany's Eifelrennen sports car race in 1936, where it won its class. Soon 328s were the car to have in sports car racing across Europe, to the point where 328s dominated sports car grids – filling the first four rows at the German Grand Prix meeting.

Works cars adopted more extreme streamlined roadster bodies for the Le Mans 24-hour race in 1938 and won their class. For the 1940 Mille Miglia the streamliner was even further developed, with a closed 'saloon' body built by Touring of Milan on their Superleggera principles, the idea being to reduce drag still further. BMW had been invited to send a team by Mille Miglia organiser Conte Aymo Maggi to ensure that his famed endurance event around Italy – which had been hit by tragic accidents and controversy – would be a proper 'international' race. Huschke von Hanstein and Walter Baumer won in their 328 saloon with more works BMWs third, fifth and sixth.

After the war 328s continued to be effective club competition cars, one notable 328 driver being a young Stirling Moss. And the powerful cross-pushrod engine would be further refined and developed by British maker Bristol to power its own range of cars, initially BMW-based, and would continue into the 1960s.

1937 BMW 328
Engine 1971cc in-line six
Bore x stroke 66 x 96mm
Valvegear Pushrod ohv
Fuel system Three Solex carburettors
Power 79bhp at 5000rpm
Suspension Front: independent, wishbones and transverse leaf spring; rear: live axle and semi-elliptic leaf springs
Wheels 16in steel disc
Brakes Hydraulic drum brakes all round
Top speed 93mph (150km/h)

Fiat 500 'Topolino'

Fiat's first 'people's car' was the 500, introduced in 1936. Its diminutive size and cheeky styling soon earned it the popular nickname 'Il Topolino' – the little mouse.

Dante Giacosa, who would be responsible for many a memorable Fiat over the next few decades, was responsible for the 500's simple engineering. Giacosa opted for a ladder chassis with its two channel-section side-members drilled to reduce weight. At the front he mounted an in-line four-cylinder sidevalve engine with an iron block and head, generating just 13bhp from its 569cc. A transverse leaf spring provided independent front suspension, while at the rear quarter-elliptic leaf springs carried a live axle.

Though it was cramped (early cars had only two seats), slow and noisy by car standards, the Topolino was a more comfortable and more practical mode of transport than a motorcycle combination. It provided essential transport for impecunious Italians, and quickly became as well-loved in its own market as the contemporary Austin Seven was in the UK.

After the war a revised 500B was introduced, the original 500 inevitably becoming known retrospectively as the 500A. The new car looked much the same, but under the bonnet it had a new overhead-valve engine, still displacing 569cc but now producing a heady 16.5bhp. It was little more than a stop-gap to a more heavily revised 500C, which followed in 1949. A full-width front end with integral headlamps modernised the Topolino, and in this form it remained in production until 1955.

Above: *Dante Giacosa gave the 'Topolino' an all-iron four-cylinder engine of 569cc, developing 13bhp. It was conventionally mounted at the front of the car.*

Below: *The cheeky appearance of the compact Fiat 500 led to the 'Topolino' nickname, which means 'little mouse' in Italian. The 500 did for Italy what the Austin Seven did for Britain.*

SS Jaguar 100

1937 SS Jaguar 100 3.5-litre
Engine 3485cc in-line six
Bore x stroke 82 x 110mm
Valvegear Pushrod-operated overhead valves
Fuel system Twin SU carburettors
Power 125bhp at 4250rpm
Suspension Front: beam axle with semi-elliptic leaf springs; rear: live axle with semi-elliptic springs
Wheels 18in knock-off wire wheels
Brakes Drum brakes all round
Top speed 100mph (161km/h)

Left: *Wide, sweeping wings and big headlamps gave the SS Jaguar 100 a rakish appearance. William Lyons himself was responsible for the highly attractive styling. A new overhead-valve cylinder head by Weslake boosted the SS100's 2.7-litre engine to 102bhp, giving the new car sparkling performance to go with its looks.*

William Lyons' Swallow company began building sidecars in 1922, and moved into cars with a special-bodied Austin Seven in 1927. By 1931 Lyons was ready to build a complete car of his own, the Standard-based SS1. The short-chassis SS90 which followed in 1935 was effectively a trial run for the SS100 a year later.

Like the earlier cars the SS Jaguar 100 had handsome lines penned by Lyons himself, with sweeping wings, cutaway doors, a folding screen and large headlamps. The big difference between them was under the bonnet. While the SS90 still used the Standard-based side-valve engine from the earlier cars, the SS100 had a new overhead valve cylinder head designed by engine expert Harry Weslake, boosting the 2.7-litre engine from 70bhp to 102bhp.

An even faster 125bhp 3.5-litre version was introduced in 1937 and it continued in production until war intervened. Both were immensely attractive and very fast, and together they did their job of raising the profile of SS in the years leading up to the Second World War. But SS concentrated on building their bread-and-butter machines, so production of the SS Jaguar 100 was never high – just 308 of all types.

The cars that would follow dropped the SS name in favour of Jaguar, which had been used as a model name since 1936 – and Jaguars would be among the most exciting classics of all.

Above: *The cramped interior is typical of a vintage sports car, as is the comprehensive instrumentation. Weather protection was rudimentary at best.*

Chapter 2

The 1940s

MG T-series

MG enthusiasts had mixed feelings about the new TA-type Midget which replaced the PB in 1936. The P-type Midgets had been stiff-riding, uncompromising sports cars with sophisticated overhead-cam engines. The TA had all the good looks of its forebears and more power, but purists looked with dismay at the Morris-influenced engineering under the skin.

The TA was longer and wider than previous Midgets, which gave it a roomier cabin, more luggage space and a larger fuel tank but meant an increase in overall weight. To offset that, it was given a larger 1292cc engine producing 52bhp – though enthusiasts were disappointed to find that the new engine was a Morris side-valve unit rather than the Wolseley-engineered overhead-cam engines of previous cars. The suspension had been softened to improve the ride quality, and the TA boasted four-wheel hydraulic brakes. It was clearly a more refined and more mature car than any of the previous Midgets.

In 1939 the Midget was given a new engine and gearbox, turning it into the TB. Flying in the face of convention the new Morris M10 engine was slightly smaller than the unit it replaced at 1250cc, but it offered significant advantages. With a shorter stroke and wider bore than before it promised better reliability, and there was a small increase in power throughout the rev range. Another benefit was the new gearbox, which used the much closer ratios of the bigger MG VA. Sadly few were made before the outbreak of war.

Above: *T-series styling gradually evolved over the years, but all the cars had separate wings and stand-up headlamps. This is the MG TD, introduced in 1948.*

Below: *Steel disc wheels were introduced on the TD, to howls of protest from enthusiasts who insisted that all proper sports cars should be fitted with wire wheels.*

In 1945 MG unveiled the TC, little more than a mildly reworked TB with a slightly wider body. Yet it was the TC which would make MG a household name not just in Europe, but also in the USA. Of the 10,000 TCs made between 1945 and 1948, just over 2000 went Stateside, many with returning servicemen who marvelled at the sheer fun to be had from the little British sports car.

The car that replaced the TC – almost inevitably known as the TD – blended the TC's traditional body style with the accomplished chassis of the Y-type MG saloon of 1947. Independent front suspension gave the Y-type excellent road manners, which were continued in the TD. Not that all MG enthusiasts approved: modern disc wheels were standard for the first time on an MG sports car, and the purists derided them.

In 1953 the TD was facelifted to produce the attractive, but still olde-worlde, TF. New rivals from Triumph and Austin-Healey soon made the MG appear archaic. Greater performance from a 1.5-litre engine helped, but the TF still looked behind the times. It took until 1955 for a truly modern MG to appear, despite the seeds having been sown as early as 1951 with a rakish Le Mans special based on the TD.

Today the TF, last of the T-series line, is one of the most highly-prized and most valuable of all MG models – thanks largely to its suave looks, which seemed so outmoded when it was new.

Above: *The double-humped scuttle and cutaway doors were characteristic features of all the T-series cars. The series continued until 1955, when the TF was replaced by the MGA.*

MG TC 1945-49
Engine 1250cc in-line four
Bore x stroke 66.5 x 90mm
Valvegear Pushrod ohv
Fuel system Two SU carburettors
Power 54.4bhp at 5200rpm
Suspension Front: beam axle and semi-elliptic leaf springs; rear: live axle and semi-elliptic leaf springs
Wheels 17in wire-spoke
Brakes Hydraulic drum brakes all round
Top speed 78mph (125.5km/h)

Lancia Aprilia

The Aprilia was the last model which Vincenzo Lancia saw taking shape before his unexpected early death in 1937. It was a clever and effective small saloon car, and a fitting epitaph.

Lancia had entered the small-car market in 1933 with the Augusta, a well-engineered compact with a 1.2-litre narrow-angle V4 engine which gave it sprightly performance. Work began on the Aprilia the following year, and the new car built on the Augusta's virtues, but added considerable innovation of its own.

Like the Augusta and Lancias before that, the Aprilia was powered by a V4 but this was a new engine, with an alloy block and a single cast iron cylinder head spanning the two cylinder banks and containing an overhead camshaft. A complex system of rockers operated the valves, allowing the head to be arranged 'cross-flow' fashion with the carburettor on one side and the exhaust manifold on the other. The running gear was unusual, too, with independent rear suspension by swing axles and a transverse leaf spring, sliding pillar independent front suspension, and inboard rear brakes.

Following aerodynamic tests at Turin Polytechnic, the Aprilia's monocoque bodyshell was given a clean, air-cleaving shape. A smooth undertray and a cabin which curved in plan and elevation both helped to minimise drag to help the Aprilia make the most of its 48bhp.

The Aprilia was famed for its superb roadholding and handling, and rightly became a popular choice for buyers wanting quality and performance in a small package. The similarly-styled but even smaller Ardea, with a 1.0-litre engine, was equally well-received, and proved that Lancia's company could survive even though its founder was gone.

Above: *The teardrop shape of the Aprilia was the result of aerodynamic testing. The underside of the car was unobstructed too, for minimal drag.*

Below: *Monocoque construction – with no separate chassis – gave the Aprilia light weight, stiffness and a spacious interior for its size.*

Lincoln Continental

1940 Lincoln Continental
Engine 4784cc 75-degree V12
Bore x stroke 73.0 x 95.25mm
Valvegear Side valves
Fuel system Single Holley carburettor
Power 120bhp at 3500rpm
Suspension Front: beam axle with transverse leaf spring and radius arms; rear: live axle with transverse leaf spring and radius arms
Wheels 16in pressed steel wheels
Brakes Drum brakes all round
Top speed 100mph (161km/h)

Left: *Edsel Ford, Henry's son, was behind the stylish lines of the Lincoln Continental. The first car was a convertible, but production cars built from 1939 on were also available in coupé form. Production was interrupted by war, but restarted in 1946. This car is a 1947 model.*

Henry M. Leland left Cadillac, the company he had founded, in 1917. He was soon back in the motor car business with a new marque, Lincoln, producing a 5.8-litre V8 saloon in 1921. But the company was not successful, and in 1922 it was taken over by Ford.

Edsel Ford, son of Henry, was by then the president of Ford Motor Company and was keen to see innovative styling and engineering alongside Ford's more conventional, mainstream products. Originally conceived as a one-off for Edsel Ford, the first Continental's stylish convertible lines caused so much interest that the car was put into production.

Just a handful were built in 1939, and then production proper began in 1940 with the Continental available in coupé and convertible forms. The bodywork was hand-crafted, and the cars were furnished in the most luxurious manner. Underneath the car borrowed the running gear from the Lincoln Zephyr saloon, with an enlarged 4.8-litre version of the Zephyr's 75-degree V12 engine.

Production was suspended once the USA entered the Second World War in 1941, but the Continental production line was restarted in 1946 and the car remained available until 1948. The Continental name was briefly revived as a brand in its own right with a brand new design called the Continental Mk 2 for 1956, but it only lasted two years. Continental then returned to the Lincoln fold as the company's top model in 1958. Continental models continued right through to 2002.

Above: *The interior of the Continental was as lavish as the exterior. The model remained on sale until 1948, and the Continental name was not used again until the mid-1950s.*

Volkswagen Beetle

Ferdinand Porsche designed a people's car for Adolf Hitler in the 1930s, when it was known as the KdF-wagen (where KdF stood for Kraft durch Freude, 'strength through joy'). Serious production did not begin until after the war, by which time the Wolfsburg factory was under British control. British motor industry experts were shown the prototype car and expressed misgivings about the design, but they were proved wrong: the 'Beetle' went on to become the best selling car ever, eclipsing the Model T Ford.

The simple formula of the 'Type 1' was based on a pressed steel platform chassis, with an air-cooled flat-four engine mounted at the back. Early cars had split rear windows and a 1131cc engine, but numerous changes and improvements were made over the years. A bigger oval rear window arrived in 1953 and featured on the popular 1200 model introduced a year later. The rear window was changed again in 1958, this time to a rectangular shape. Bigger engines followed, a 1285cc unit in 1965 and a 1493cc, 44bhp engine in 1966.

The 'Super Beetle' of the 1970s introduced MacPherson strut front suspension, disc front brakes, a rounded nose providing more luggage space and the debut of a curved windscreen. Throughout the Beetle's career – which continued in South America after German production ended in 1980 – there was an attractive convertible option, and these are now the most sought-after Beetles of all.

Above: *Ferdinand Porsche mounted the VW's air-cooled flat-four engine in the tail. Note the split rear window on this 1947 car.*

Below: *The 'Beetle' shape changed little over the years. It became familiar the world over, as the VW eclipsed the Ford Model T's sales record.*

Allard

London-based Sydney Allard built a trials special in the 1930s using a Ford Pilot V8 engine and chassis, with divided-axle independent front suspension and a simple open two-seater body. After the war Allard went into production, though numbers were always limited.

In the 1940s Allard produced a variety of related models. The J1 was a short wheelbase two-seater with lightweight competition bodywork, while the K1 was slightly longer and more accommodating and the L longer still and fitted with four seats – although it was still not the most practical of cars.

The M1 had a more practical body and a two-door saloon, the P1, followed. Sydney Allard himself used one to win the Monte Carlo Rally in 1952, proving that the performance was still there even if some of the cars were becoming more civilised. But Allard still catered for those who wanted out-and-out performance with cars like the stark J2.

Ford V8 power was standard Allard wear but in Britain a 3.9-litre Mercury unit was a performance option. In the US Allards were powered by Cadillac, Oldsmobile or Chrysler V8s giving the cars amazing acceleration.

As the 1950s wore on Allard introduced more sophisticated models with coil-spring front suspension and more modern styling. But the company struggled to compete with the likes of Jaguar, which could produce cars in much greater numbers and undercut many specialist manufacturers on price while offering similar performance. By 1959 Allard cars had ceased production.

Top and above: *The first Allards were trials specials, but in the 1950s the cars became gradually more sophisticated and market-friendly. Allard's home-market cars usually employed Ford or Mercury V8s, but in the US Cadillac, Oldsmobile and Chrysler units were used.*

Above: *Most Allards were stark two-seaters with simple bodywork, but four seaters and saloons were also built.*

Triumph 1800/2000 Roadster

Standard's Sir John Black rescued the moribund Triumph car company during the war and introduced new models in 1946. The staple product was the 1800 saloon, a staid but handsome device with razor-edge styling, independent front suspension and hydraulic brakes.

The Roadster, introduced the same year, followed a similar pattern. Its chassis was the same as the saloon's, retaining the transverse leaf-spring independent front suspension and leaf-sprung live axle rear. The engine was the same, too, a long-stroke 1776cc four derived from the Standard 14 unit, delivering 65bhp. The difference was all in the bodywork, which was an attractive two-door drophead hiding a 'dickey seat' in the tail, its flip-forward cover incorporating a windscreen for passengers.

In 1948 both the saloon and the Roadster adopted the 2088cc Standard Vanguard engine (which, in tuned form, would power Triumph TR sports cars in the 1950s and 1960s). The result was a little more power, but unfortunately the Vanguard engine came with a decidedly unsporting three-speed gearbox, so even in its later form the Roadster had little sporting appeal.

What it did have was handsome styling – the front end, with its big chrome headlamps, imposing grille and curvaceous wings was especially attractive – and luxurious accommodation, with a wide cabin offering space for three in the front.

Production of the Roadster ended in 1949, though the saloon continued until 1954, latterly sharing the Standard Vanguard chassis.

Much later the Roadster became familiar to TV audiences in Britain as the car of choice for Jersey-based detective Bergerac, played by John Nettles.

1949 Triumph 2000 Roadster
Engine 2088cc in-line four
Bore x stroke 85 x 97mm
Valvegear Pushrod-operated overhead valve
Fuel system Solex carburettor
Power 68bhp at 4200rpm
Suspension Front: wishbones and transverse leaf spring; rear: live axle with semi-elliptic springs and anti-roll bar
Wheels 16in steel-disc wheels
Brakes Hydraulic drum brakes all round
Top speed 82mph (132km/h)

Below: Triumph's 1800 Roadster was based on the 'razor edge' 1800 saloon. Both cars were introduced in 1946, with the British motor industry barely recovering after the war. Attractive lines, rather than all-out performance, were the Roadster's strength. Later cars were fitted with a 2088cc engine. The car pictured is a 2000 Roadster of 1949.

Bristol 400-406

BMWs car designs were acquired by Bristol as war reparations. The British company – an offshoot of the famous Bristol aircraft and aero-engine firm – took the best bits of BMW's pre-war output and combined them into an effective new car. Bristol put its aircraft engineering skills to good use, employing its expertise in materials science and its painstaking attention to detail to revise the stylish BMW 327 two-door saloon body, the 326 chassis and the 328's cross-pushrod engine, which when brought together produced the Bristol 400 of 1947.

The 400 was succeeded by the aerodynamically-shaped 401 in 1949, which sired a rare drophead, the 402. Actor Stewart Granger and his wife Jean Simmons had a matching pair of 402s. The 403 of 1953 was similar, but featured a host of detail revisions and more power, together with a remote gearchange lever on final versions.

The Bristol's BMW roots were harder to spot when the styling was revised for the short-wheelbase two-door 404 and long-wheelbase four-door 405. The distinctive air intake in the nose was said to mimic those on the ill-fated Bristol Brabazon airliner. Both cars still used the BMW-derived cross-pushrod six and torsion-bar suspension.

The engine was expanded to 2216cc for the disc-braked 406, which had a larger, squarer bodystyle but retained a resemblance to its predecessors from the front. A handful of 406s were bodied by Zagato, as sporting two-door coupés.

Bristol now needed more power than its ageing 2.2-litre six could provide, and for the 407 of 1961 the company turned to Chrysler V8 engines. These would continue to serve Bristol into the next century.

Above: *Bristol became a car manufacturer using reworked BMW designs. The 402 is a rare drophead version of the 1949 401 saloon.*

Above: *Aerodynamic performance and well-sorted handling were always Bristol strong suits. This model is a 404.*

Aston Martin Two-Litre Sports (DB1)

David Brown bought Aston Martin in 1947, after seeing the company advertised in the classified columns of *The Times* newspaper. Brown had been impressed by a wartime Aston prototype, the Atom, which provided the basis for the first true post-war model.

Brown wanted the new car to be a drophead, so chief engineer Claude Hill redesigned the chassis, using twin side tubes to make up for some of the stiffness lost by removing the fixed roof. An anti-roll bar was added to the front suspension, and at the rear the leaf springs were replaced by coils, trailing arms and a Panhard rod. A new body was designed by Frank Feeley, chief designer at the Lagonda company – another David Brown acquisition.

The car was launched as the Aston Martin Two-Litre Sports at the London Motor Show in 1948. Despite valuable publicity from Aston's surprise win in the Spa 24-hours with a racing version of the same chassis, just 14 production cars were sold – largely because the hand-built Aston could not compete on price with the new Jaguar XK120, launched at the same show.

Aston Martin quickly moved on to a new car powered by a six-cylinder Lagonda engine, which would make its debut in motor racing before being adapted for the road. That was the DB2, a name which led to the earlier car being retrospectively dubbed the DB1.

Above: *Frank Feeley designed the handsome lines of the Two-Litre Sports, known retrospectively as the DB1. The chassis underneath had been developed in the Atom prototype during the war.*

Below: *Aston Martin's first post-war design was the Two Litre Sports, which was later dubbed the DB1. Just 14 were built before the car was replaced by the DB2.*

Jaguar XK120

Above: The Jaguar XK120's styling was fresh and new in 1948. The car caused a sensation when it was unveiled at the London Motor Show.

1949 Jaguar XK120
Engine 3442cc in-line six
Bore x stroke 83 x 106mm
Valvegear Twin overhead camshafts
Fuel system Twin SU carburettors
Power 160bhp at 5000rpm
Suspension Front: wishbone and torsion bar; rear: live axle with semi-elliptic springs
Wheels 16in wire or steel-disc wheels
Brakes Hydraulic drum brakes all round
Top speed 125mph (201km/h)

Above left: As ever, William Lyons was personally involved in the XK120's styling. The shape was continued in the XK140 and XK150 models.

Jaguar caused a sensation at the first post-war London Motor Show in 1948. War-torn Britain was still suffering from rationing, and had just endured one of the coldest winters anyone could remember. Yet Jaguar's stand at the Earls Court show revealed a breathtaking new sports car, the XK120, which promised to deliver exceptional performance at a remarkably affordable price.

Its role was two-fold. First, the XK120 was a show-stopping attention-getter to raise Jaguar's profile as it introduced a series of important post-war saloon cars. Second, the XK120 allowed Jaguar to prove the all-new XK engine in a low-volume car before using it in a mainstream saloon.

The 3.4-litre XK engine was a classic in-line six-cylinder unit with twin overhead camshafts, said to develop 160bhp in its initial form. The car it powered was built on a chassis related to that of the new MkV saloon, but shorter and lighter, and at first clothed in aluminium alloy bodywork. Steel-bodied production cars came on stream in 1950.

The first XK120s were dropheads, but a fixed-head coupé was added to Jaguar's lineup in 1951, the same year that the competition-orientated XK120C (better known as the C-type) was revealed.

In 1954 Jaguar unveiled the XK140, a more powerful and better-handling vehicle but perhaps lacking a little of the XK120's styling purity. The XK150 of 1957 was even more a grand tourer, with more interior space, greater luxury and more power to offset increased weight.

The XK line continued until 1961, when it was replaced by another Jaguar sensation, the E-type.

Above: The twin-cam XK engine, initially used in 3.4-litre form, would be used by Jaguar for decades to come.

Morris Minor

Above: Monocoque construction gave the Minor a spacious interior for a car its size.

Alec Issigonis, who would later create the BMC Mini, was also the brains behind the Morris Minor. And given a freer hand the Minor could have been just as revolutionary: Issigonis' early plans included the use of front-wheel drive and a flat-four engine, but cost considerations forced the adoption of rear-wheel drive and an existing power unit, the 918cc side-valve engine from the Morris Eight Series E.

Even so, on its introduction in 1948 the Minor was a very modern design. The conventional separate chassis was gone, Issigonis combining the load-bearing members into the floor of the pressed-steel bodyshell in a 'unitary' structure. Issigonis designed the Minor with front-biased weight distribution, giving excellent stability in all conditions. Even the styling was innovative, with the headlamps set low in the front of the car.

Sadly new safety legislation forced Morris to raise the Minor's headlights in 1949. A four-door model followed in 1950, then the Series II cars appeared in 1952 with their 803cc Austin engines. In 1954 the 'cheesecutter' grille gave way to the more familiar horizontally-slatted type, and a new dashboard modernised the interior. The Morris 1000 of 1956 had the larger 948cc A-series engine, and a new single-piece curved windscreen – though, curiously, the Post Office Minor vans retained the old 803cc engine until the early 1960s. The millionth Minor was built in 1960, with a run of lilac-coloured 'Minor Millions' to celebrate. The last major update was the fitment of the 1098cc engine in 1962, after which the Minor soldiered on almost unchanged. Production of saloons ended in 1971, but the light commercials were still produced until 1974.

Below: Excellent roadholding and stability made the Minor a safe and predictable car, but early models had minimal performance thanks to their aged side-valve engines.

Porsche 356

1960 Porsche 356 Super 90
Engine 1582cc air-cooled flat-four
Bore x stroke 82.5 x 74mm
Valvegear Pushrod-operated overhead valves
Fuel system Twin Zenith carburettors
Power 90bhp at 5500rpm
Suspension Front: trailing arms and torsion bars; rear: swing axles, radius arms and transverse torsion bars
Wheels 15in steel wheels
Brakes Hydraulic rum brakes all round
Top speed 115mph (185km/h)

Above left and above: *The prototype 356, built in late 1947, looked similar to the production cars but was significantly different in its mechanical layout and structure.*

Porsche started work on the first car to be marketed under its own name in 1947. The prototype 356 carried its 1131cc Volkswagen-based engine amidships in a tubular spaceframe chassis and was clothed in hand-beaten aluminium panels, but by the time serious production got under way in 1949 the design had been revised with a rear-mounted engine and a platform chassis carrying a pressed-steel body.

Early cars were built at Porsche's workshops in Gmünd, but production moved to Stuttgart in 1950. Gradually the 356 was developed, with ever larger engines, first a bored-out 1300 and then a long-stroke 1500 with a built-up roller-bearing crankshaft. In 1954 Porsche introduced the 356 Speedster which lacked some of the usual 356 equipment but was lighter, faster and also cheaper – inevitably it sold well. In 1955 numerous revisions were incorporated in the 356A.

The same year Porsche introduced a high performance version of the 356, known as the Carrera. The extra performance came from a 100bhp 1498cc engine with twin overhead camshafts per cylinder bank, an engine already a success in Porsche's 550/1500RS racing car.

Further revisions, including a taller and wider bodyshell, produced the 356B of 1958, powered by 1582cc engines with 60bhp, 75bhp or 90bhp. The last of the line was the 356C of 1963, with retuned suspension and all-round disc brakes. By then work was already under way on the 356's successor, the iconic 911.

Above: *The simple dashboard of the Porsche 356 prototype presented only essential information to the driver. The car's white plastic steering wheel would hardly be considered 'sporting' today.*

Chapter 3

The 1950s

Bentley MkVI/ R-Type/Continental

Rolls-Royce and Bentley formulated a rationalisation plan just before the war, the first fruits of it being the MkVI Bentley introduced in 1946. The substantial cruciform-braced chassis with independent front suspension were those of the short-lived MkV, mated with the new B60 'F-head' engine of 4257cc developing 137bhp. For the first time in-house 'Standard Steel' bodywork was available.

Though its appearance was sedate, the new Bentley's road manners were anything but. Calls for more fashionable bodywork came from the continent, and a low-line chassis with a more laid-back steering column rake was clothed in full-width bodywork by Pininfarina to produce the rare Cresta, built by Jean Daninos' Facel-Metallon company. The same chassis was also developed for a high-performance Bentley with a lightweight two-door body by H.J. Mulliner. It was called the Continental, and was unveiled in 1952. With a higher compression ratio and a special low-loss exhaust system – which gave a distinctive growl – the Continental was the fastest four-seater production car of its era.

For 1953 the MkVI was superseded by the R-Type, with a larger boot and a more powerful 4566cc engine. The Continental was upgraded with a 4887cc engine, and continued in production until 1955. Just 207 production cars were built (plus a single prototype, known as 'Olga') making the Continental the most sought-after classic Bentley of all.

***Above:** The sought-after Continental was based on the MkVI's chassis, fitted with lightweight low-drag bodywork and a more powerful engine. Just 208 were built between 1952 and 1955.*

***Below:** Bentley's MkVI offered excellent ride and handling and a typically conservative appearance. With an enlarged boot and larger, more powerful engine the R-Type of 1953 was an even more attractive package.*

Aston Martin DB2

The second new Aston Martin to appear after David Brown's acquisition of the company, the DB2, was first seen in 1949 at the Le Mans 24-hour race. Two of the three entries were powered by the 2.0-litre four-cylinder engine used in the DB1. The third was fitted with the 2.6-litre LB6 engine, which Brown had recently acquired along with the rest of the ailing Lagonda company.

That Le Mans race was an unhappy and unsuccessful one for Aston Martin – one car finished seventh, but the 2.6 retired with mechanical failure and the third crashed, killing its driver. But the DB2 proved its potential with a fine third place finish in the Spa 24-hours the following month. The production two-seat DB2 was launched at the New York motor show in April 1950.

The DB2 quickly became the best-selling car Aston Martin had ever made. A drophead was introduced in 1951, and then in 1953 Aston Martin announced the DB2/4 with the addition of small rear seats and a lift-up rear luggage door.

A Mark II DB2/4 with a slightly higher roofline was introduced in 1955, by which time the car was powered by a 3.0-litre version of the LB6 engine. More engine development was evident in the Mark III of 1957: Polish engineer Tadek Marek had redesigned the unit, which offered 162bhp as standard and 214bhp in 'competition' specification.

The popular Mark III continued until 1959, when Aston Martin introduced an important new model – the DB4.

Above: *The DB2/4 was the four-seater, three-door version of the DB2 introduced in 1953.*

Above: *The second of David Brown's Aston Martins introduced the famous grille shape which persists to this day.*

Jaguar C-type/D-type/XKSS

Fast though it was, the Jaguar XK120 was never likely to be a serious threat to the purpose-built Ferraris and Cunninghams in sports car racing. To meet the challenge Jaguar planned a lightweight racing machine with a sleek aluminium body, powered by a tuned XK engine. It was to be called the XK120C, 'C' for Competition, but soon became known as the Jaguar C-type.

Unlike the XK120 with its box-section steel chassis, the C-type used a very stiff tubular steel structure to form the centre of the car, with a lightweight subframe carrying the wishbone front suspension and the 200bhp twin-carburettor engine. The live rear axle was suspended by torsion bars and braking was by big drums front and rear.

The C-type made its Le Mans debut in 1951, where two of the three cars entered were sidelined with engine failures but the third, driven by Peter Walker and Peter Whitehead, won convincingly.

Jaguar put the C-type into limited production in 1952 and reappeared at Le Mans that year with special streamlined cars. But the low-drag bodywork led to engine overheating, which put the C-types out of the race. More successful was the debut of disc brakes on the C-types at the Mille Miglia, and in 1953 Jaguar was back at the front with C-types first, second and fourth at Le Mans.

A new car, the D-type, was readied for 1954. Like the C-type it was based around a stiff central structure, but instead of a tubular frame the D-type had a stressed-skin monocoque similar in concept to advanced aircraft designs. The

Below: *The Jaguar XK120C or C-type was a purpose built sports racing car which built on the competition success of the XK120 road car, and continued such success at Le Mans.*

Left: The driver, once installed in the D-type's snug cockpit, was reasonably well protected by a wrap-around plastic windscreen.

Above: Aerodynamicist Malcolm Sayer shaped the bodywork of the D-type Jaguar. Low drag, with the Le Mans' long Mulsanne straight in mind, was the aim.

Above: The XKSS was a road-going version of the D-type, with a road-car windscreen and hood. Just 16 were completed before the production line was destroyed by fire.

familiar XK engine was mounted at the front, now incorporating dry-sump lubrication to reduce the height of the tall unit and improve oil feed to the bearings in race conditions. With the long Mulsanne straight at Le Mans firmly in mind the new car was given a gorgeous low-drag body designed by aircraft aerodynamicist Malcolm Sayer.

The D-type could only manage second place on its Le Mans debut in 1954, but Mike Hawthorn and Ivor Bueb won in 1955 – though only after the Mercedes-Benz cars were withdrawn following the accident which killed Mercedes driver Pierre Levegh and 80 spectators. In 1956 the works cars failed but the Ecurie Ecosse team, using ex works D-types, came through to win and they repeated the success in 1957.

Earlier that year a major fire at Jaguar's Coventry factory had ended the career of a road-going derivative of the D-type, before it had really begun. The XKSS was intended to be the ultimate Jaguar road car, and also a useful tool for American production sports car racing. It was effectively a D-type with a full windscreen, tiny bumpers, indicators and a rudimentary hood. Just 16 were built before the fire destroyed the production line.

The C-type and D-type Jaguars are today some of the best-loved of all classic competition cars, and command enormous sums when they come up for sale – particularly those with interesting competition records. There's a whole industry based on building replicas, usually using later versions of the long-running XK engine rescued from a rusting XJ6 saloon. But there's nothing quite like the real thing.

1955 Jaguar D-type

Engine 3442cc in-line four

Bore x stroke 83 x 106mm

Valvegear Twin chain-driven overhead camshafts

Fuel system Three twin-choke Weber carburettors

Power 285bhp at 5750rpm

Suspension Front: wishbones and torsion bars; rear: live axle with trailing arms and torsion bars

Wheels 6.50-16in alloy

Brakes Hydraulic disc brakes all round

Top speed 176mph (283km/h)

Lancia Aurelia

Another innovative Lancia. Vittorio Jano gave the Aurelia a new 60-degree, all-alloy V6 displacing just 1754cc and deploying its 56bhp through a transaxle (a gearbox in unit with the rear axle). The engine was subsequently enlarged to 2.0 litres and 2.2 litres, the latter giving 87bhp. Suspension was independent all round, at first with coils and semi-trailing arms at the back but from 1954 adopting a leaf-sprung De Dion setup.

Just under 13,000 Aurelia saloons were built between 1950 and 1955, but other derivatives continued until 1958. The B20 GT coupé with its beautifully simple Pininfarina body and a twin-carb, 1991cc version of the V6 was first seen in 1951. With 75bhp (soon boosted to 80bhp in the Second Series versions) and excellent roadholding, the B20 GT was an effective competition car. For 1952 Lancia introduced a 2.5-litre, 110bhp Third Series, often called the 2500GT. Like the saloon, the GT adopted De Dion rear suspension in 1954.

At the same time the Spider was introduced, a drophead designed and built by Pininfarina on a shorter wheelbase. The Spider had a wrap-around, American-style, windscreen, but for 1956 it was replaced by a Convertible fitted with a conventional screen and quarterlights.

The Aurelias are fast, good-handling cars from a time when Lancia was a credible independent manufacturer. Though rust is a perennial problem and restoration costs can be steep, Aurelia values remain high, particularly for the rarer GT (3871 made), Spider (240) and Convertible (521).

Above: *Lancia's Aurelia saloon was an innovative machine with a new all-alloy V6 engine. The coupé version was introduced in 1951.*

Below: *The Aurelia coupé was a beautiful road car and an effective competition machine. Ultimately it was fitted with a 110bhp 2.5-litre engine and De Dion rear suspension.*

Austin-Healey 100

Above: *The Austin-Healey cleverly re-used existing Austin mechanicals in a stylish roadster body. Four-cylinder models like this were followed by the six-cylinder 100/6 and 3000.*

Donald Healey's Austin-based sports car, the Healey Hundred, was famously adopted by Austin overnight at the London Motor Show: it swiftly became the Austin-Healey 100.

Healey's clever re-use of rather mundane Austin mechanicals produced a tough, capable sports car that performed well but didn't cost the earth. The original 100, with a 2660cc four-cylinder engine from the woefully dull Austin Atlantic, was originally mated to an existing four-speed gearbox which had its too-low first gear blanked off to produce a three-speeder with reasonable ratios. Double overdrive also helped, and a proper four-speed (plus overdrive) 'box followed in 1955.

Higher performance versions of the Austin-Healey inevitably followed. The first of them was the 100M with a high-compression engine developing 110bhp. Even faster was the desirable 100S introduced in 1954, fitted with an alloy-head version of the Austin engine generating 132bhp, along with lightweight alloy panels and disc brakes. Just 55 100S models were built.

In 1956 the four-pot car was replaced by the six-cylinder 100/6 (which led to the earlier car being retrospectively referred to as the 100/4). Early 100/6s all offered two-plus-two accommodation, but the two-seater wasn't completely dead: a version was reintroduced in 1958. Though more refined than before the 100/6 was slower than the four-cylinder cars it replaced, a situation not rectified until the advent of the Austin-Healey 3000 in 1959.

1953 Austin-Healey 100
Engine 2660cc Austin in-line four
Bore x stroke 87.3 x 111.1mm
Valvegear Pushrod-operated overhead valves
Fuel system Twin SU carburettors
Power 90hp at 4000rpm
Suspension Front: wishbones, coil springs and anti-roll bar; rear: live axle with semi-elliptic springs
Wheels 16in wire wheels
Brakes Hydraulic drum brakes all round
Top speed 115mph (185km/h)

Chevrolet Corvette 1953-62

Though they pioneered a brand that's still going strong today, the first Corvettes were under-engineered, under-powered and unpopular. The idea was to provide a home-grown American answer to the influx of European sports cars, from the MGs and Triumphs at the bottom end to the Jaguar XK120 further uprange. Style was the major attraction, the glassfibre body penned by Harley Earl's team hitting every one of the 1950s dream-car hot spots from the wrap-around screen and cowled headlamps to the two-place cockpit and glitzy dashboard. Early cars had a prosaic 3.8-litre six with just 150bhp, but V8s soon came on stream to offer a small but welcome boost in performance.

For 1956 the Corvette was heavily restyled with four headlamps, scalloped sides and a twin-bulge bonnet aping the Mercedes-Benz 300SL. Under the skin there were big changes, too, with bigger V8 engines (up to 5.4 litres) offering as much as 360bhp. For the first time that gave the Corvette the straight-line speed to match its looks: the original straight-six cars could barely exceed 100mph (161km/h) but late '50s V8s were good for nearly 140mph (225km/h). Up against tidy-handling European opposition the Corvette's brakes and suspension were nothing to write home about, but careful development gradually improved the handling to the point where the Corvette became competitive in production sports car racing.

All Corvettes have a strong following, but for the most part they're available in reasonable numbers. Not so the early 1950s versions, and that rarity makes them the most valuable classic Corvettes of all.

Above: *The first-generation Corvette is a fascinating piece of '50s nostalgia, though it was less popular than expected when it was new.*

Below: *Whitewall tyres and wrap-around windscreen point to the Corvette's 1950s origins. Early cars had pedestrian 3.8-litre six-cylinder engines with 150bhp.*

Sunbeam Alpine

The Sunbeam Alpine was introduced in 1953, but the story really began two decades earlier with the launch of the 1.2-litre Hillman Minx in 1935. After the war the Minx was rebodied and relaunched as the Sunbeam-Talbot Ten. Revised styling and an overhead valve 2.0-litre engine turned the Ten into the much more attractive Sunbeam-Talbot 80 and 90 models in 1948. A 2267cc engine was adopted in 1950, turning the 90 into an 85mph (137km/h) car, and by 1953 the engines had been tuned still further, and the brakes enlarged.

An open two-seater version followed the same year. Stirling Moss had proved his versatility by winning the famous Alpine rally in a 90, so the Alpine name was adopted for the new sports car.

The styling followed the same lines as the saloon, though there were louvres on the bonnet to allow hot air out and to hint at the high-compression 2267cc four underneath. A straight-through exhaust helped boost the power output to 80bhp, and there was higher-geared steering and a stiffer chassis to aid handling. Though the hefty chassis and saloon-derived body meant it was heavy, limiting its nimbleness and blunting performance, it was an appealing package.

Minor improvements were made to the saloon and the Alpine in 1954. Though the saloon continued to be built into 1957, the Alpine was dropped in 1955 after about 3000 had been made. It proved to be a tough and capable rally car, and played a starring role alongside Cary Grant and Grace Kelly in the Alfred Hitchcock film *To Catch a Thief*.

Above: *The Sunbeam Alpine roadster was based on the 80 and 90 saloons. It was a tough and capable rally car.*

Below: *The snug interior has space for two. The large-diameter white plastic steering wheel is a typical '50s touch.*

Triumph TR2/3

Triumph revealed a prototype of a new sports car at the London Motor Show in 1952. Though that car, the 20TS, never made it into production a heavily revised version did, in 1953.

Called the TR2, it had a longer version of the 20TS's stub-tailed two-seater body and a ladder-frame chassis with wishbone and coil independent front suspension. It was powered by a linered-down version of the Standard Vanguard in-line four-cylinder engine, with a capacity of 1991cc. Fitted with twin carburettors it provided 90bhp. The result was a tough, reliable sports car with a reasonable turn of speed.

An improved version, the TR3, went on sale in 1955, and in 1956 front disc-brakes were specified – the first volume-production car to have them. Power rose to 100bhp for the TR3a of 1957, and the nose was restyled with a full-width grille. From 1959 there was the option of a 2138cc engine.

When the bigger Michelotti-styled TR4 of 1961 came along with its modern full-width styling and wind-up windows, that should have been the end of the road for the 'sidescreen' TR3a. But strong demand from the American market for the traditional TR led Triumph to reconsider, and an export-only version continued to be made into 1962, alongside the new car. This was later dubbed the TR3b.

These sidescreen TRs were a major success for Triumph, more than 80,000 of them finding buyers between 1953 and 1962. They're still fun to drive, and because the spares situation is good and there are some excellent Triumph clubs to help out if things go wrong, they make sound classic buys.

Above: *In 1956 the TR3 became the first volume-production car to be fitted with disc front brakes. The flush front grille differentiates the TR3 from the TR2.*

Below: *Triumph's head of engineering, Ken Richardson, took a modified TR2 to a record 124mph (199km/h) flying mile on the Jabbeke highway in Belgium in 1953. Even the standard car was good for over 100mph (161km/h).*

Alfa Romeo Giulietta/Giulia Sprint/Spider

Strapped for cash after the war but in need of a vital new mid-range saloon model, Alfa Romeo came up with a novel plan to fund development of its new car: a lottery, with examples of the new saloon, the Giulietta, as the prizes. But development dragged on and on, and with no cars to award to the lucky winners Alfa Romeo seemed to be on the verge of a public relations catastrophe. The answer was to commission a coupé that could be put into production quickly using a body built by Bertone: the Giulietta Sprint was born.

The Sprint combined a typically lithe and well-balanced Bertone shape with the performance created by the new 1.3-litre twin-cam engine, which would be an Alfa staple for decades to come. It was a huge success.

An equally pretty convertible, the Giulietta Spider, came along in 1955 and provided Alfa Romeo with another instant hit. The following year an uprated engine with higher compression and more aggressive cam profiles became available in the Sprint and Spider Veloce.

A 1570cc version of the twin-cam engine provided a small increase in power and more importantly a considerable boost in mid-range torque for the Giulia Sprint and Spider launched in 1962. The Spider was also available in Veloce form with still more power – 112bhp – and latterly both Sprint and Spider were given front disc brakes. The Spider outlived the Sprint by a year, ending its run in 1965.

Above left: *The pretty Giulietta Spider was introduced in 1955 alongside the Sprint coupé. It continued in production a year after the Sprint was discontinued.*

Above and below: *Both Bertone and Zagato produced special-bodied versions of the Sprint. Zagato's was the stub-tailed SZ, this is Bertone's Giulietta Sprint Speciale.*

Facel Vega

1962 Facel Vega Facel II
Engine 6286cc 90-degree Chrysler V8
Bore x stroke 108.0 x 85.9mm
Valvegear Pushrod-operated overhead valves
Fuel system Single Carter carburettor
Power 355bhp at 4800rpm
Suspension Front: wishbones, coil springs and anti-roll bar; rear: live axle with semi-elliptic springs
Wheels 15in centre-lock steel wheels
Brakes Disc brakes all round, servo assisted
Top speed 133mph (214km/h)

Jean Daninos' Facel (Forges et Ateliers de Construction d'Eure et Loire) company built car bodies for French manufacturers, and Daninos was always keen to create a 'Grand Routier' in the tradition of the now-defunct Delage and Delahaye marques from before the Second World War. In 1948 Facel built bodies for the rare Bentley Cresta, and Daninos had the last Cresta-specification chassis clothed with a modern new coupé body in 1951. It was an attractive body style, and one that would reappear in a revised form on Facel's own car, the Facel Vega FV of 1954.

Under the stylish skin, with its stacked headlamps and dog-leg windscreen, power came from a lusty 4.5-litre Chrysler V8, which gave the Facel Vega excellent performance. Even more performance was available from the revised HK500 model of 1957, with up to 360bhp from a 6.3-litre V8. Power steering and automatic transmission were available to take the strain out of driving, and from 1960 there were disc brakes on all four wheels to make sure the stopping power was up to the task of bringing this heavy GT car to a halt.

Facel had introduced a stretched four-door, the Excellence, in 1956, but it sold only in small numbers. The 1.6-litre Facellia, powered by Facel's own twin-cam engine, proved more popular but did not sell in the numbers hoped for. In 1961 the HK500 was replaced by the restyled Facel II, and in 1963 the Facellia gave way to the Volvo-engined Facel III. But it was too late: Facel was wound up in 1964.

Below: The attractive styling of Facel Vega cars was descended from builder Jean Daninos' own special-bodied Bentley of 1951. These handsome cars were built from 1954 to 1964. With effortless power from Chrysler V8 engines, power steering and automatic transmission, the Facels were ideal cars for trans-continental motoring.

Ferrari 250GT/GTO

The first road-going Ferraris were built in the late 1940s, although they were thinly-disguised racing machines. It wasn't until the 250GT appeared in 1954 that the cars were built in appreciable numbers.

All the 250s used a 2953cc version of the V12 designed by Gioacchino Colombo, the '250' name referring to the (approximate) capacity of one cylinder. Early 250GTs had 200bhp and could reach 120mph (193km/h). The elegant touring bodies were by Pininfarina, which was already established as Ferrari's preferred bodywork designer.

The rare 250GT Tour de France, with a tuned engine giving up to 280bhp, followed in 1955 and cabriolet versions of the 250GT were available from the end of 1957. More significant was the introduction in 1959 of a short wheelbase version with 8in (200mm) chopped out of the middle of the car, stiffening the chassis and improving the handling. They were an effective weapon in production sports car racing.

In 1962 the long-wheelbase 250GT was discontinued and the short-wheelbase car turned into the more comfortable and better-equipped 250GT Berlinetta Lusso. Meanwhile, for racing, Ferrari produced a lighter, more aerodynamic version called the 250GTO. Just 39 of these fantastic machines were built, but Ferrari fans the world over recognise their curvaceous low-drag bodywork in an instant.

The touring 250GT Lusso was now producing 240bhp, while the racing GTO was up to 300bhp. In an effort to improve power still further the V12 was bored out from 73mm to 77mm, taking its capacity up to 3286cc. The result was the 275 series, which replaced the 250 in 1964.

Above and below: *Ferraris were only produced in small numbers until the mid-1950S when the 250GT arrived. This is a rare 205GT Tour de France, with a tuned engine developing 280bhp. The 250 series continued until 1964.*

Mercedes-Benz 300SL

Mercedes-Benz dominated European sports car racing in 1952, finishing second on its debut in the Mille Miglia and then winning at Le Mans, the Nürburgring and in the South American Carrera Panamericana. The successful car was a lightweight coupé designed by Rudolf Uhlenhaut, known internally as W194. It took its engine and suspension from the existing 300 saloon and mounted them in a lightweight spaceframe chassis, clothed in a wind-cheating alloy body. Conventional doors were impossible because of the chassis design, so lift-up 'gullwing' doors were provided instead. The world soon knew it as the 300SL, the letters standing for 'sports lightweight'.

For 1953 Uhlenhaut planned a series of improvements to the SL, including bigger wheels and tyres, a new form of swing-axle rear suspension and fuel injection for the 3.0-litre straight-six engine. But before the revised car could appear in competition Daimler-Benz management turned its focus away from sports cars to Formula 1 Grand Prix racing.

That might have been the end of the SL, had it not been for Austrian émigré Max Hoffman, importer of Mercedes-Benz cars to the US. Legend has it that Hoffman told Daimler-Benz management that if they built a road-going 300SL he could sell a thousand of them, and backed up his argument with a down-payment.

The production car used the new fuel-injected engine and a slightly longer version of the spaceframe chassis, but reverted to the conventional swing-axle rear suspension of the earlier racing SLs. It was also given a steel body with

***Below:** The 300SL Roadster was easier to drive and an easier machine to live with than its 'gullwing' coupé predecessor.*

Left: *'Gullwing' doors were dictated by the shape of the spaceframe chassis. Modifications allowed conventional, but heavier, doors on the Roadster.*

Above: *The 300SL Roadster (left) and coupé are two of the most glamorous cars ever to wear the Mercedes-Benz star.*

Above: *The 300SL's dramatic shape was largely the result of aerodynamic testing, a legacy of its origins as a sports-racing car. Even the 'eyebrows' over the wheelarches were functional, separating the airflow along the side of the car to help keep the windows clean in bad weather.*

aluminium opening panels, resulting in a significant increase in weight. Racing SLs had been comfortably trimmed but the road car was even more luxurious, and was given a tilting steering wheel to aid entry and exit. The new car made its debut at the International Motor Sports Show in New York in January 1954.

Production began later that year and continued until 1957, by which time nearly 1400 examples of the 'gullwing' SL had been built. It was replaced by a 300SL Roadster, but the folding top and the conventional doors with their wind-down windows were just part of a package of changes which made the new version far easier to live with.

The spaceframe chassis was revised with lower sills to accommodate the normal doors, and extra bracing was introduced into the front bulkhead and above the transmission tunnel to restore the lost stiffness. Though the modifications were effective, they added about 220lb (100kg) to the weight of the car. Engine revisions produced an increase in power to compensate. Another significant change was the adoption of the low-pivot swing-axle design, which improved the Roadster's on-the-limit handling.

Nearly 1900 Roadsters were built between 1957 and 1963, alongside more than 25,000 of the much cheaper – but visually similar – 190SL. Both were replaced by another Uhlenhaut masterpiece, the 'Pagoda roof' 230SL of 1963. By then the 300SL had established itself as a favourite of the rich and famous: filmstars Tony Curtis and Sophia Loren, King Hussein of Jordan, comedian Tony Hancock and jazz pianist Oscar Peterson all had them. The 300SL was the car to be seen in.

1954 Mercedes-Benz 300SL 'Gullwing'
Engine 2996cc in-line six
Bore x stroke 85 x 88mm
Valvegear Single chain-driven overhead camshaft
Fuel system Direct fuel injection
Power 215bhp at 5800rpm
Suspension Front: double wishbones, coil springs, telescopic dampers, anti-roll bar; rear: swing axle, coil springs, telescopic dampers
Wheels 5x15in steel disc
Brakes Hydraulic drum brakes all round
Top speed 161mph (259km/h)

Ford Thunderbird

Ford's answer to the Chevrolet Corvette was less a sports car, more a fast touring machine. 'A new high-spirited personal car that's at home on boulevard… or open road,' said a sales brochure at the time. The Thunderbird was first seen as a prototype at the Detroit Auto Show early in 1954, and production T-birds started to roll off the lines later that year.

V8 engines from the start ensured that the straight-line performance was better than the 'vette, whether you specified the 'Fordomatic' auto transmission or the three-speed manual with automatic overdrive. There was effectively only one body, an open two-door two-seater with a removable glassfibre hard top. A power-operated folding hood was a popular option.

For 1956 the spare wheel was mounted externally to improve boot space and the hard top was given 'porthole' side windows. The standard 292ci (4785cc) V8 was joined by a high-performance 312ci (5113cc) option. The T-bird was restyled for 1957 with a new grille, revised bumpers and bigger rear fins, and there was a rare supercharged engine option.

The last of these 'Little Birds' was built in December 1957. The car that replaced them was a bigger, four-seater machine with boxy styling which led to its nickname of 'squarebird'. Successive generations of T-birds just kept getting bigger and heavier – and further away from the concept that made the original such a classic. Ford acknowledged that fact with the introduction in 2002 of a new generation of Thunderbirds with throwback styling – which inevitably acquired the nickname 'retro bird'.

Above: *The Thunderbird was Ford's answer to the Chevrolet Corvette. It was a fast tourer with impressive performance thanks to big V8 engines.*

1955 Ford Thunderbird	
Engine	4786cc 90-degree Ford V8
Bore x stroke	95.3x 83.8mm
Valvegear	Pushrod-operated overhead valves
Fuel system	Single Holley carburettor
Power	198bhp at 4400rpm
Suspension	Front: wishbones, coil springs and anti-roll bar; rear: live axle with semi-elliptic springs
Wheels	15in steel wheels
Brakes	Drum brakes all round, servo assisted
Top speed	115mph (185km/h)

Below: *There was only one T-bird body, an open two-door with a removable glassfibre top. This early car lacks the porthole side windows that were added to the hardtop in 1956.*

BMW 507

American importer extraordinaire Max Hoffman was behind the BMW 507. When the V8-engined 502 saloon was introduced in 1954, Hoffman suggested building a sports car around the new engine. He also introduced BMW to Count Albrecht von Goertz, a German designer now resident in the US.

Goertz designed two V8-engined cars for BMW, a handsome two-door model available in coupé and cabriolet forms known as the 503, and an aluminium-bodied sports car – the 507. Fitted with a 150bhp version of the 3.2-litre V8 and capable of nearly 140mph (225km/h), the 507 had the performance to justify the exotic looks Goertz had given it. The 507 had a litheness and elegance to its lines which contrasted sharply with the over-detailed, chrome-laden excesses of Detroit at the same time, and it reflected Goertz' belief that simplicity and restraint were the way to a timeless and effortlessly attractive shape.

Hoffman had told BMW he'd order 2000 507s provided that the purchase price would be 12,000 Deutschmarks. Sadly the 507 went on sale at nearly double that, which meant a US list price edging towards $9000 at its launch, and as a result a very limited clientele. Just 254 were built between 1957 and 1959, the last few with disc front brakes and even higher prices. Today that makes the 507 the rarest and most desirable BMW of its era, and one of the greatest 1950s classics of all.

Above and below: *The clean, elegant lines of BMW's 507, by Count Albrecht von Goertz, were a refreshing change from the chrome-clad excess offered by America's major manufacturers in the 1950s. Thanks to high prices the V8-engined 507 remained a rarity.*

BMW Isetta

Renzo Rivolta's company Iso started out making refrigerators, then branched into scooters and utility three-wheelers. In 1953 Iso developed the tiny bubble-shaped Isetta four-wheeler, just 89in (2260mm) long, intended to provide the next step up from a scooter. It had a single door across the nose, carrying the top mounting of the steering column so that the steering wheel hinged out of the way when the door was opened. Power came from a 236cc two-stroke twin, mounted low down at the rear.

BMW's own range was concentrated at the luxury end of the market, and it needed a volume product, so Munich bought the rights to the Isetta and fitted it with the four-stroke 247cc single-cylinder engine from the R25 motorcycle, launching the BMW Isetta 'Motocoupe' at the 1955 Frankfurt motor show. A 297cc Isetta 300 followed in 1956, and later that year the body was revised with larger side windows. BMW made more than 161,000 of what Germans called 'the rolling egg' in eight years. A few thousand more were built under licence in Britain, where they had a single rear wheel to take advantage of the cheaper road tax on three-wheeled vehicles.

The Isetta idea was developed into the BMW 600, with a larger body and 585cc version of the long-running BMW boxer motorcycle engine. Nearly 35,000 were built but the 600 never sold as well as BMW hoped: it simply didn't have the Isetta's cheeky appeal.

Above: *BMW's version of the Isetta was powered by the 247cc single-cylinder engine from the R25 motorcycle. This is a three-wheeled UK variant.*

Below: *A single door across the nose of the Isetta provided access to the interior. In Germany the car's shape led to the nickname 'rolling egg'.*

Chrysler 'Letter Cars'

The horsepower race which all America's major manufacturers were fighting to win at the end of the 1960s really began back in 1955 with Chrysler's C-300. C stood for coupé, and the 300 indicated that this luxury hardtop had a 300bhp version of Chrysler's famous 'hemi' V8. Even more power was on tap for its replacement, the 300B, in 1956. Out went the 331ci (5424cc) engine and in came a 354ci (5801cc) unit with 340bhp in standard form and 355bhp in high-compression guise.

Virgil Exner's aggressive 300C for 1957 was available both as a hardtop and a convertible. To go with the new styling there was, of course, more power, 375bhp from the standard 392ci (6424cc) hemi. The 1958 300D was much the same, with mildly updated styling and engine revisions taking the output up to 380bhp. For the 1959 300E the 'hemi' was replaced by the wedge-chamber Golden Lion V8 engine, offering the same power output from a larger (413ci, or 6768cc) but lighter engine.

The loss of the legendary 'hemi' hurt sales, but Chrysler was back in business in 1960, offering an optional 400bhp 'short ram' engine in the 300F – though only a handful were built, complete with four-speed Pont-á-Mousson manual gearboxes, as used on the Chrysler-powered Facel Vegas. In the 1961 300G a three-speed Chrysler manual gearbox took the place of the French unit.

Slow sales of the 300H (1962) and 300J (1963) led Chrysler to cut the price for the 300K, which became the best-selling of the letter cars. The last of the line was another best-seller, the '65 300L.

Above: *Chrysler's 'letter cars' were some of the first American 'muscle cars'. All shared aggressive styling and potent V8 engines.*

Above: *The letter cars started the horsepower race which dominated the American motoring scene in the 1960s. Power ranged from 300bhp in 1955 to over 400bhp by the mid-1960s.*

Citroën DS/ID

Few cars caused such a stir on their launch as did Citroën's replacement for the Traction Avant, the DS. It looked like nothing on earth in 1955 and that organic, aerodynamic shape still seems like it belongs to a car of the future 50 years later. Under that remarkable skin the DS was no less impressive, with powered hydraulic systems to raise, lower or level the suspension, assist the steering and transmission and power the brakes. The DS could even jack itself up to make tyre changing easy.

The Achilles heel was found under the bonnet, where the DS carried forward the old long-stroke four-pot engine that had served Citroën since the 1930s. New motors didn't arrive until the mid-'60s, and as the DS aged larger engines and fuel injection were made available to keep its performance competitive.

Variants included the simpler ID, luxury DS Pallas, the rare and elegant Chapron-built Décapotable (drophead) and the vast Safari estates (with three rows of seats in Familiale trim). In France the DS was used for everything from a taxi to a presidential limousine, in the latter case saving de Gaulle's life thanks to its ability to make a rapid getaway despite bullet-damaged tyres after an assassination attempt.

The entry-level ID was replaced by D Special and D Super models in 1969, while at the other end of the range the ultimate 2.3-litre fuel-injected, five-speed DS23 arrived in 1972. The DS continued until 1975, when it gave way to the equally futuristic CX.

1955 Citroen DS19

Engine 1911cc in-line four

Bore x stroke 78.0 x 100.0mm

Valvegear Pushrod-operated overhead valves

Fuel system Single Weber carburettor

Power 75bhp at 4500rpm

Suspension Front: leading arms and anti-roll bar; rear: trailing arms; hydro-pneumatic system with front/rear interconnection and self-levelling

Wheels 400mm steel wheels

Brakes Inboard disc front, drum rear, high pressure hydraulic assistance

Top speed 88mph (142km/h)

Below left and below: *Dramatic styling inside and out announced Citroën's replacement for the Traction Avant. The DS was unconventional in the extreme, but it offered remarkable comfort and driving ease. It would remain in production for two decades.*

MG MGA/Twin Cam

Above: *The attractive MGA sports car was a long time coming, but it proved to be a huge success for MG with more than 100,000 built between 1955 and 1962.*

By the early 1950s MG was part of the British Motor Corporation (BMC). Though MG would eventually benefit from the Corporation's resources, in the early days the men at Abingdon struggled to press ahead with vital new models because BMC management had pet projects elsewhere.

One such was the Austin-Healey 100. While a new marque was being born and a new sports car sent to America to earn export sales, MG was told to do no more than revamp its increasingly old-fashioned T-series line. By the time the final T-series model, the TF 1500, went on sale in 1954, it looked very much like yesterday's car.

Replacement finally came in 1955, with a shape which had been seen as far back as 1951, when an MG TD with full-width low-drag bodywork had appeared at Le Mans. The shape had been further refined in the EX175 prototype of 1953.

The production MGA was first available as a roadster and then, from 1956, as a coupé. At first it was powered by a 1489cc BMC B-series with 72bhp, but in 1958 a 1588cc twin-cam unit with 108bhp was also offered. The Twin Cam – which proved to be unreliable unless treated carefully – had disc brakes all round and centre-lock Dunlop wheels.

In 1959 the standard MGA engine was enlarged to 1588cc and in 1961 it grew again to 1622cc for the MGA Mk2, recognisable by grille bars which were recessed instead of flush-fitting. Production continued until 1962, by which time more than 100,000 had been built. The MGA was a huge success for Abingdon, and remains a well-loved classic.

Below: *The MGA Twin Cam developed 108bhp, though reliability was sometimes lacking. Note the Jaguar D-type-like Dunlop centre lock wheels, standard on the Twin Cam.*

Chevrolet Bel Air

The Bel Air headed up Chevrolet's model range from 1953. It was a premium model targeted at affluent young drivers, giving them performance and clean-cut style in a big value package.

In 1955 GM restyled the Bel Air and introduced a V8 engine option to give it a straight-line speed boost. The new unit was the 'small block' V8 which would become a legendary performance engine, and would be built in its millions over the next five decades.

The high point came in 1957. In an era of fins and chrome where too much was never enough, the '57 Bel Air was more restrained than most, with a well-proportioned shape and trademark hooded headlamps. Though saloons and estates were available, the most sought-after (then as now) were the hardtop coupé and convertible. Options included seat belts or shoulder harnesses, hood ornaments and a vertical spare wheel carrier. Top of the list of engine choices was the Turbo-Fire V8 with Ramjet fuel injection, said to offer one horsepower for each of its 283 cubic inches of displacement.

The '58 Bel Airs were wider, longer and heavier than before and some of the magic had been lost. Though the Bel Air line would continue into the 1970s, it would gradually drop down Chevrolet's pecking order as higher-spec models (such as the Impala and Caprice) were introduced. For many, the late '50s Bel Airs, and the '57 in particular, are the ultimate classic Chevys.

Above: *The big steering wheel, chrome horn ring and column gearchange are all classic 1950s automobile features.*

Below and bottom: *The 1950s Bel Airs ('57 left, '56 right) are some of the best-loved of all classic Chevys.*

Lotus Elite

Racing car constructor Colin Chapman's first proper road car was true to Lotus' core values: light, agile, fast and technically advanced. Sadly it could also be fragile, and because of its higher cost of manufacture it wasn't the financial success that Chapman had hoped for.

The Elite was a monocoque design in an era when separate chassis were still common, but what made it even more unusual was that the entire body/chassis unit was made from glassfibre reinforced plastic. The spectacularly pretty styling, by John Frayling, was also very efficient aerodynamically. Suspension was all-independent, by wishbones and coils at the front and struts at the rear. Disc brakes were fitted all round, the rears inboard.

A race-derived all-alloy engine from Coventry-Climax provided the power, at first about 71bhp from just four cylinders and 1216cc. The 1960 Special Equipment model was tuned to give 85bhp and also had a close-ratio ZF gearbox. The Super 95, Super 100 and Super 105 models came in for further tuning, which increased power to as much as 105bhp.

It was a compelling package, though not always a reliable one. Quality control of the bodyshells was sometimes lacking (not least because Lotus chose cheaper suppliers over better ones) and the Coventry-Climax engine could be somewhat temperamental if maintenance was skipped.

In the end a little over a thousand Elites were sold. The model was replaced in 1963 by the Elan, which promised more performance and more reliability thanks to a steel backbone chassis and a bigger-capacity twin-cam engine based on Ford components – and also offered the option of a convertible body.

Above: *The Elite's styling, by John Frayling, was deceptively simple but effortlessly beautiful. The body was a glassfibre monocoque. Coventry-Climax engines with up to 105bhp powered the Elites, and thanks to the suspension design know-how of Lotus boss Colin Chapman the handling and roadholding of these cars were unbeatable.*

1963 Lotus Elite SE

Engine 1216cc in-line four

Bore x stroke 76.2 x 66.6mm

Valvegear Single chain-driven overhead camshaft

Fuel system Twin SU carburettors

Power 85bhp at 6300rpm

Suspension Front: wishbones, coil springs and anti-roll bar; rear: struts, fixed-length driveshaft links and radius arms

Wheels 15in wire wheels

Brakes Discs all round, inboard at rear

Top speed 118mph (190km/h)

Edsel

Most classics are remembered because they were innovative, or stylish, or successful in competition, or because they sold in volume. Ford's 1957 Edsel can't claim any of those distinctions: it's remembered today as probably the biggest marketing disaster in the history of the motor car.

The Edsels – named after Henry Ford's son, who died from cancer in 1943 – were conventional 1950s American fare, full-size separate-chassis saloons, hardtops, convertibles and estates. Engines were V8s at first, from 4.8 litres to 6.7 litres, though there was a poverty-model 3655cc, 147bhp straight-six in 1959. So far so good – but there were problems.

The first problem was the styling. 'No other car looks like the Edsel' ran a billboard campaign, but the trouble was nobody wanted any car to look like that. The huge vertical grille was dismissed as a 'horse collar', and among the more polite comments was the suggestion that the Edsel looked 'like a Mercury pushing a toilet seat'.

The Edsels also had to contend with an economic downturn just as they were launched. The Edsel ranges – Ranger, Pacer, Corsair, Citation and the Bermuda, Villager and Roundup estates – were intended to sit between the bargain-priced Fords and mid-range Mercurys. But with the American economy in tatters Ford dealers offered big discounts to keep stocks moving, and suddenly a well-equipped Fairlane looked like good value compared to an ugly Edsel – and competitors were discounting just as hard. In such uncertain times customers started looking for smaller cars, and ignored Edsels in their thousands.

Ford pulled the plug in 1959 after three seasons during which the Edsel lost around $300 million.

Top: *Ford's Edsel offered its owners standard 1950s driver comforts, including auto transmission and power steering.*

Above: *The 'horse collar' grille was one of the Edsel's biggest problems – it simply wasn't a style people liked.*

Below: *Edsels were available in several trim levels and body styles during their three-year life – but even the convertibles were unpopular.*

Austin-Healey Sprite

BMC boss Leonard Lord came up with the idea for the Sprite, telling Donald Healey that he wanted a modern version of the popular Austin Seven 'Nippy' models of the 1930s – a small, fun, sports car based on existing production components where possible to keep it cheap and easy to maintain.

Geoffrey Healey laid out the new car, which was styled by Healey body designer Gerry Croker. Originally the headlamps were intended to be buried flush in the bonnet and raised when in use, but cost considerations led to the adoption of the fixed 'frogeye' (or 'bugeye' in the US) lamps which gave the car its nickname. Under the steel bonnet – which extended right down to the sills on either side – sat a twin-carburettor version of the ubiquitous Austin A-series engine, in 948cc form.

The frogeye Sprite ran from 1958 to 1961. The Mk2 Sprite which replaced it was given a styling makeover: incredibly, the Healeys reworked the nose while MG at Abingdon restyled the tail! MG's almost identical Midget ran alongside the Sprite from 1961. A 1098cc engine and disc front brakes were adopted in 1962, and in 1964 the outwardly similar Mk3 Sprites were given wind-up windows, locking doors and semi-elliptic rear springs in place of the original cantilever quarter-elliptics. The Sprite MkIV (and Mk2 Midget) from 1966 introduced a 65bhp 1275cc engine and a folding (rather than removable) hood. Sprite (and Midget Mk3) production ended in 1971, the last few badged as Austins rather than Austin-Healeys to avoid paying royalties to the Healey family…

Above and below: *The tiny Austin-Healey Sprite was based on mundane Austin parts but offered enormous fun behind the wheel. This is an early frogeye (or bugeye) Sprite.*

Cadillac Eldorado

General Motors' styling chief Harley Earl was the man who gave America fins, and the height – literally – of the craze came in 1959 with one of Earl's last cars, the Cadillac Eldorado.

The '59 Eldorado epitomises classic American automobiles: it's a vast, V8-powered, chrome-laden cruiser with the accent firmly on style and luxury. Even today elements of the specification wouldn't sound out of place on a luxury car: air suspension, an automatic transmission, and power operation for the brakes, steering, seats, windows, door locks and the huge folding top. But delve deeper into the data and it's obvious that this is a car of the 1950s.

Power, for instance, comes from a huge, 6390cc V8 engine which may deliver a gross output of 345bhp, but still relies on pushrods to operate the valves and has given its all well before 5000rpm. Despite all that power acceleration is adequate rather than astonishing and the top speed is only 110mph (177km/h), thanks to an all-up weight in excess of two tonnes and laughable aerodynamic performance. The brakes given the task of hauling this heavyweight down from 100mph (161km/h) or more may be feather-light to use, but they are fade-prone drums. Fuel consumption can easily dip below 14mpg.

None of that really matters, because the Eldorado is an icon of '50s America. Few cars are more recognisable, or more accurately reflect the dreams and aspirations of their era. The Eldorado, too, represents the beginning of the end of Detroit's love of ostentation and excess: within five years, fins would be dead.

Above: *Eldorado was the glamorous full-size convertible at the top of the Cadillac range in the 1950s. Few cars make such a bold statement about their owner, even today.*

Below: *The '59 Eldorado was the height – literally – of the fins craze. The chrome laden styling might polarise opinion, but there's no denying it as an icon of '50s America.*

Mini

Above: *The Mini's transverse engine, front-wheel drive layout set the pattern for small cars which endures today. The potent Mini-Cooper became a successful race and rally car.*

The 1956 Suez Crisis led to the revival of interest in bubble cars, but BMC boss Leonard Lord had a better idea. Chief engineer Alec Issigonis was instructed to produce a proper small car, not a superannuated motorcycle combination. Lord's only stipulation was that Issigonis had to power the car with an existing BMC engine.

Only one engine was anything like suitable: the A-series unit which powered the Austin A35 and A40 Farina, and which had boosted the performance of the (Issigonis-designed) Morris Minor in the Minor 1000 of 1956. Issigonis mounted the engine sideways at the front of his new car, driving the front wheels through a gearbox which sat under the engine, sharing its oil supply. The resulting drivetrain was incredibly compact, which meant that the overall size of the car could be kept small while still offering useful interior space. Issigonis saved further space by badgering Dunlop to produce tiny 10in tyres.

At the 1959 launch the car was badged as the Morris Mini-Minor and the Austin Seven, but soon they were all just known as 'Minis' and the Austin and Morris badges were eventually dropped in 1969.

The Mini's excellent roadholding and handling were exploited to the full when racing car constructor John Cooper dropped a Formula Junior specification engine into one to produce the Mini-Cooper, an instant saloon car race winner and the most successful rally car of its era.

Despite regular reports of its imminent death, the Mini soldiered on and on, the last car being built in October 2000. More than five million were made.

1963 Morris Mini Cooper S
Engine 1071cc in-line four, transversely mounted
Bore x stroke 70.6 x 68.3mm
Valvegear Pushrod-operated overhead valves
Fuel system Twin SU carburettors
Power 70bhp at 6000rpm
Suspension Front: wishbones and rubber springs; rear: trailing arms and rubber springs
Wheels 10in steel wheels
Brakes Disc front, drum rear, servo assisted
Top speed 95mph (153km/h)

Chapter 4

The 1960s

Aston Martin DB4/5/6

These are the most influential Aston Martin models ever made. Their style and the strategy behind them has echoed down through the years, and still has a bearing on the products made by the very different Aston Martin company of today.

They stemmed from company owner David Brown's desire to take on – and beat – the best that Ferrari could offer. That meant building a car styled by the greatest designers in the world, and offering levels of performance greater than anything Aston Martin had previously produced.

Polish engineer Tadek Marek came to Aston Martin to design a new 3.7-litre six-cylinder engine, while Aston chassis engineer Harold Beach created a new steel platform chassis in consultation with the Carrozzeria Touring styling house. Touring penned a lithe and elegant fastback body to be built using their 'Superleggera' construction method where aluminium panels are supported by a lightweight tubular framework.

The DB4, as it was called, was launched at the London Motor Show in 1958. Though early cars were plagued by lubrication problems the DB4 was a huge success, selling faster than any previous Aston. Once the fixed-head coupé was in production a drophead was developed, and customers could specify more powerful 'Special Series' engines with three twin-choke Weber carburettors in place of the usual SUs.

Above: *Tadek Marek's twin-cam straight-six engine, in various sizes and levels of tune, powered every one of the DB4/5/6 family of Aston Martins.*

Below: *The DB4 body was styled by Carrozzeria Touring and built using the company's Superleggera construction method, which proved both light in weight and elegant.*

1963 Aston Martin DB5
Engine 3995cc in-line six
Bore x stroke 96 x 92mm
Valvegear Twin chain-driven overhead camshafts
Fuel system Three SU carburettors
Power 282bhp at 5500rpm
Suspension Front: wishbones and coil springs and anti-roll bar; rear: coil-sprung live axle with trailing arms and Watts linkage
Wheels 15in wire wheels
Brakes Hydraulic disc brakes all round, servo assisted
Top speed 143mph (230km/h)

In 1960 a racing derivative, the DB4 GT, was introduced. With a five-inch shorter wheelbase, just two seats, and a tuned twin plug engine the DB4 GT proved to be a handsome and effective sports racing machine. Even more handsome, to many eyes, was the rare Zagato-bodied version which was lighter and even quicker.

A revised version of the DB4's chassis and an enlarged 4.0-litre version of its engine went into a new Lagonda, the Rapide, in 1961. In 1963 the revised engine found its way back into the Aston, which now incorporated numerous tweaks and improvements and was known as the DB5. The prototype DB5 (actually a late DB4 Vantage) was one of two cars used in the James Bond film *Goldfinger*, presenting Aston Martin with huge publicity in 1965.

By then Aston Martin was already planning to introduce a further revision of the same car, the DB6. Though this looked bigger and heavier than the DB5 there was actually little to choose between them: it was an optical illusion caused by the DB6's higher roofline, which gave more headroom to rear seat passengers. The DB6 continued until the end of 1970, latterly running alongside the new Aston Martin DBS and DBS V8 models.

Above left: *'Volante' had long been the name associated with open-top Astons, but the drophead DB5 is correctly called a DB5 Convertible.*

Below: *The higher roofline of the DB6 improved headroom in the rear, while the reshaped tail improved stability at speed.*

Austin-Healey 3000

The six-cylinder Austin-Healey 100/6 was more refined and more grown-up than the original four-cylinder 100, but enthusiasts were disappointed to learn that it was also a shade slower. Even the later versions with six-port cylinder heads and more power struggled to outpace the earlier cars. Those looking for a faster Healey had to wait until 1959, and the introduction of the Austin-Healey 3000.

As its name implies, the 3000 was fitted with a (nominally) 3.0-litre engine in place of the 2.6-litre unit in the 100/6 – actually a 2912cc straight-six developing 124bhp. Disc front brakes, now becoming common on performance cars, were also fitted. Like the 100/6, the 3000 was available in two-seater and two-plus-two forms, though most buyers opted to have the extra seats.

The next significant development was the MkIIa, which introduced a curved windscreen, wind-up windows instead of removable side screens and a fold-down hood instead of the earlier removable affair. The gentrification of the 'Big Healey' continued with the MkIII of 1964, which was given a more luxurious interior featuring a wooden dashboard, and a brake servo to lighten pedal pressures – but also had a 148bhp engine for swifter performance.

The big Healeys were a major sales success, attracting thousands of enthusiasts in the home market – where the cars' many rally victories kept them in the public eye – and tens of thousands more in the US. Today these are fondly remembered and eagerly sought cars which command premium prices.

Above: The 3000 was the ultimate Austin-Healey, with the usual stylish lines and a 3.0-litre six-cylinder engine.

Below: The 'Big Healey' proved to be a popular road car and a consistent rally winner, driven by the likes of Timo Makinen, Pat Moss and the Morley brothers.

Chevrolet Corvair

Rising sales of imported cars in the late 1950s, spearheaded by the Volkswagen Beetle, convinced US manufacturers that they had to offer 'compact' cars alongside their full-size products. In 1959 Chevrolet unveiled its offering in the compact class, the Corvair – available as a four-door saloon, a two-door hardtop or a two-door convertible. The Corvair was unusual because of its unitary construction, rear-mounted engine (an air-cooled flat-six) and all-independent suspension.

The suspension would prove to be its Achilles heel. At the rear the Corvair used a simple swing-axle arrangement, which was tricky to handle in extreme situations, and the anti-roll bars which might have improved matters were omitted to reduce production costs. Instead the recommended front tyre pressures were kept low in an effort to reduce the Corvair's tendency to oversteer, but uninformed mechanics often raised the pressures thinking they were too low.

Ralph Nader's famous book *Unsafe at Any Speed* pilloried the Corvair's handling and destroyed any real chance the car had for success, despite changes to the rear suspension in 1964: a transverse camber-compensating leaf-spring was added, and this tamed the handling to a degree.

A further step came in 1965 when the Corvair adopted the better-located independent rear suspension from the Corvette. At the same time the bodywork was restyled with crisper, cleaner lines which turned the Corvair from a curiously-proportioned ugly duckling into something of a looker. But it was still not enough to make a real success out of Chevrolet's unconventional compact. Production ended in 1969.

Above and below: *Chevrolet's Corvair was an unconventional compact car with a rear-mounted air-cooled flat-six engine and all-independent suspension. Handling worries limited its success, despite improvements to the rear suspension on later models which cured the problems.*

Daimler SP250 Dart

Daimler built a reputation for conservative luxury saloons, and for many years enjoyed royal patronage for its grandest products. In 1959 it went after a very different type of customer by building a new two-seater sports car for the lucrative American market. Originally it was to have been called the Daimler Dart, but following objections from Chrysler (which used the Dart name under its Dodge brand) the car was renamed the SP250.

Then as now, the Daimler SP250's styling divided opinion. The glassfibre-bodied two-seater roadster – an unusual market for Daimler – was certainly distinctive, but a lot of people couldn't get past that rather fish-like face or the self-conscious flowing lines moulded into the flanks above the wheels. Those who could see past the looks revelled in the engineering under the skin.

The SP250's trump card was under the bonnet, a 2548cc V8 engine designed by Edward Turner of Ariel and later Triumph motorcycle fame – by this time Triumph and Daimler were both owned by the BSA group. Turner's superb engine gave the SP250 excellent flexibility and 120mph (193km/h) potential.

Early SP250s suffered from flexible chassis (leading to tales of doors coming open during hard cornering) and cracking bodywork. After Jaguar's takeover of Daimler in 1960 the SP250 was reworked with a stiffer chassis and stronger bodyshell, which addressed many of the criticisms – but did nothing about the dubious styling. Jaguar, however, was concentrating on fulfilling demand for the 1961 E-type and the popular Mark 2 saloons (including the Daimler V8-250 with Turner's V8 engine). The SP250 fell by the wayside in 1964.

***Above and below:** Edward Turner's magnificent 2.5-litre V8 engine gave the SP250 sports car decent pace and excellent drivability. But dubious looks and the takeover of Daimler by Jaguar meant a short production run for the Dart which ended in 1964.*

Jaguar Mark 2

Above: *A classic shape, lusty performance and six-cylinder refinement made Jaguar's Mark 2 saloons very popular in the 1960s.*

Jaguar launched a new range of compact saloons with the 2.4 in 1955 and 3.4 in 1957. Power came from the usual XK straight-six engines, but the structure was an all-new monocoque bodyshell. In 1959 Jaguar launched a revised car, which was simply called the Mark 2.

The thick door frames and small windows of the earlier cars made way for stylish chrome window frames and a much larger glass area, giving the Mark 2 a fresh, modern appearance and a much lighter and more inviting cabin. In addition to the 2.4 and 3.4 engines there was now a 3.8-litre unit, with which the Mark 2 was good for 125mph (201km/h). Revised rear suspension with wider track improved grip, and as a result there was little to match the 3.8 Mark 2's blend of straight-line speed, cornering and accommodation.

It dominated saloon car racing and also became a favourite of armed robbers, who stole 3.8s wearing car club badges wherever possible, because they were usually the best maintained.

In 1963 the Mark 2's structure was mated with the independent rear suspension of the E-type to produce the S-type, which ran alongside the Mark 2 until 1968. The Mark 2 body was also given the Daimler Dart engine to produce a compact Daimler saloon, the 2.5-litre V8.

All Jaguar's compact saloons were replaced in 1968 by the XJ. Almost four decades later the Mark 2 – luxury saloon performance car, race winner, getaway car – is one of the best-loved of all Jaguars.

1959 Jaguar 3.8 Mark 2

Engine 3781cc in-line six

Bore x stroke 87.0 x 106.0mm

Valvegear Twin overhead camshafts

Fuel system Twin SU carburettors

Power 220bhp at 5500rpm

Suspension Front: wishbones and coil springs; rear: live axle with trailing links and cantilever leaf springs

Wheels 15in steel or wire wheels

Brakes Disc all round, servo assisted

Top speed 125mph (201km/h)

Sunbeam Alpine/Tiger

The Alpine name, dormant since 1955, reappeared on a new two-seater sports car in 1959. The monocoque body shared its floorpan with nothing more exciting than the Hillman Husky, a utilitarian Minx derivative. But the styling was sharp (with prominent fins on early cars) and there was a twin-carb 1494cc to provide reasonable performance. In 1960 the Alpine was upgraded with a 1592cc engine, and the following year a fastback coupé version built by Harrington was approved by Sunbeam's parent company Rootes as an official model. Three distinct types were offered between 1961 and 1963, all of them rare.

In 1963 a host of detail improvements were made to the Alpine including revised suspension, better seats, quarter lights and an optional hardtop. The fins were trimmed in 1964, and the final cars built from 1965 to 1968 gained a 1725cc twin-carb engine with 92.5bhp.

If you wanted more power than that, you needed a Sunbeam Tiger – effectively an Alpine fitted with a 260ci (4261cc) Ford V8 engine developing 164bhp, turning it into a 120mph (193km/h) motor car. The Tiger II of 1967 offered even more pace, thanks to a larger 289ci (4727cc) Ford Mustang engine with 200bhp. But the Tiger was killed off in its prime, in 1968, after Rootes was taken over by the American Chrysler company. Chrysler objected to the use of a Ford engine in one of its products, and Chrysler's own V8 wouldn't fit.

Both the Alpine and Tiger are underrated cars, lacking the image of flashier MG, Triumph and Austin-Healey rivals. As classic sports cars go, they're bargains.

Above: *Comfortable interiors were a feature of both the Alpine and the V8-engined Tiger.*

Below: *Until 1964 Alpines had pronounced fins at the rear, as was then the fashion. They were toned down on later cars.*

Volvo P1800

Above left: *First and last of the breed, the P1800 coupé (front) and the three-door 1800ES estate (rear). The P1800 series was in production for more than a decade.*

Above: *Volvo neatly developed the 1800E into the ES estate by extending the roofline and adding a glass tailgate.*

Volvo was well known for building strong, reliable saloons, though it had dabbled in the sports car market in 1956 with the short-lived P1900. The Swedes jumped back into the sports car business with a much more serious effort, the P1800, in 1960.

The attractive two-door coupé body was styled by Frua, and built by Pressed Steel in Scotland. The shells were then sent to West Bromwich, Birmingham, where they were trimmed and painted by Jensen. Unfortunately quality was poor and the process expensive – Jensen spent a lot of time rectifying transit damage to the shells – and in 1963 Volvo moved the production line to Sweden. At the same time the engine was tuned to produce 108bhp, and the model renamed 1800S. The distinctive 'cowhorn' bumpers were deleted in 1964. In 1968 a 2.0-litre engine was installed and with fuel injection (in the 1970 1800E) it was good for 130bhp, producing a top speed of 115mph (185km/h).

Following the success of Reliant's Scimitar GTE, Volvo created its own 'sporting estate' based on the 1800E. The 1800ES, as it was called, had an extended rear roofline and glass tailgate and ran from 1971 to 1973.

The P1800 and its successors are best remembered for their starring role in the 1960s TV series *The Saint*, with Roger Moore playing Simon Templar. The producers of the programme had wanted a Jaguar E-type, but at the time Jaguar was selling all the cars it could build, and refused to help. Volvo jumped at the chance to supply cars for the series – always white, Templar's trademark colour – and Moore liked them so much he had one of his own.

Above: *Volvo's tough four-cylinder engines were used in twin-carb form, latterly with fuel injection and 130bhp.*

Ford Falcon

Above: Though the Falcon was a 'compact' car by American standards, there was still plenty of room inside.

After recession hit the US economy in the late 1950s, car buyers started to demand smaller 'compact' cars, and the Falcon was Ford's response. Smaller than the established Fairlane saloon, but still big enough to fit the family and everything it needed to haul, and fitted with a 144ci (2360cc) six-cylinder engine giving comparatively good fuel economy, the Falcon was just the right car at just the right time. It quickly became one of Ford's best sellers.

In 1963 the Falcon went in a new direction, with the introduction of a 164bhp, 260ci (4261cc) V8 engine option. To publicise this new 'Falcon Sprint' Ford entered a team of three cars in the tough Monte Carlo Rally, prepared by Holman and Moody, and run from England by Jeff Uren. Anne Hall's car was delayed by bad weather, Swede Bo Ljungfeldt's recovered from clutch problems to win the final stages and finish 43rd overall, while Peter Jopp's Falcon managed 35th overall and won its class.

Eight Falcons were entered in the 1964 Monte Carlo Rally, with glassfibre body panels to reduce weight and 305bhp 289ci (4736cc) engines. All eight cars successfully finished the rally, and this time Ljungfeldt brought his car home in second place overall.

But the popularity of the Falcon Sprint had already peaked. The stylish new Ford Mustang was taking over, and when a new Falcon was introduced in 1965 it was a bigger car based on a shortened Fairlane platform. And the rallying days of Ford's V8-powered American cars were over.

1963 Ford Falcon Sprint
Engine 4261cc 90-degree V8
Bore x stroke 96.5 x 72.9mm
Valvegear Pushrod-operated overhead valves
Fuel system Single two-barrel carburettor
Power 164bhp at 4400rpm
Suspension Front: wishbones, coil springs and anti-roll bar; rear: live axle with leaf springs
Wheels 14in steel wheels
Brakes Drum brakes all round, servo assisted
Top speed 107mph (172km/h)

Below: The Falcon Sprints competed in the Monte Carlo Rally in 1963 and 1964, then had a famed career in British saloon car racing in red-and-gold Alan Mann colours in the hands of Frank Gardner.

Ford Galaxie

One of the best known of the full-size American cars of the 1950s and 1960s, the Galaxie line began in 1959 but really started to make an impact with an award-winning restyle for 1961. It was available in a wide range of models, from the Club saloon to the Starliner convertible, and there were also huge estates on offer.

The pattern was repeated in 1962 with 14 models on offer, including new 500XL luxury hardtops and convertibles with bucket seats and chromed door inlay panels. That year engine options ranged from the six-cylinder 'Mileage Maker' to the triple-carb 'Super High Performance' V8 with 405bhp.

The Galaxie reached its peak in 1963 with a bold new body style and even greater performance. A rare option was Ford's high-performance 427ci V8, packing no less than 425bhp. Tuned Galaxies soon started to appear in saloon car racing in the UK, where they had the power to out-drag the previously dominant Jaguars from a standing start – though they struggled to keep up with the smaller cars on the narrower, twistier circuits. The '63 Galaxies also saw the introduction of a new pillarless fastback body option.

In 1965 a brand new bodystyle was introduced to the Galaxie line – its principal features being stacked headlamps and an aggressive front end. It lasted until 1967, when it was replaced by a new model with hidden lamps. But these later cars looked more anonymous than the earlier models and it is the pre-'68 Galaxies which enthusiasts look out for. The most eagerly sought of all are the high-performance '63 models.

Above: *Galaxie fans include Lord March, the organiser of Britain's greatest historic race event – Goodwood Festival of Speed. This is his 1963 Galaxie on the Goodwood circuit.*

Below: *The many Galaxie options included an enormous convertible, which Ford dubbed the Starliner. This is a 1964 500XL.*

Jaguar E-type

The E-type is an icon of the Swinging Sixties, and it isn't difficult to see why. Sensational looks, the ability to reach close to 150mph (241km/h), and all for half the price of an Aston or a Ferrari: Jaguar's sports car was an instant sensation.

Its curvaceous good looks – equally good in roadster and fixed-head forms – were clearly related to the Le Mans-winning D-types of the 1950s, sculpted by aerodynamicist Malcolm Sayer. Its structure was similar too, with a monocoque central tub and a tubular front section carrying the engine and front wheels – though the exotic aluminium and magnesium alloys of the D-type were replaced by steel. The E-type's engine was also shared with previous models, a 3.8-litre development of the fine straight-six XK unit with a claimed 265bhp. Wishbones and torsion bars provided independent suspension at the front, and the rear was also independently suspended by lower wishbones, fixed-length driveshafts and twin coil spring/damper units.

Jaguar claimed a top speed of 150mph (241km/h), which road tests subsequently proved – though the test cars had been carefully prepared and, in truth, production cars fell slightly short of the mark. Although production E-types weren't quite as quick, they were still as rapid as almost any competitor and much cheaper than most. The model soon became a regular in sports car racing, and Jaguar built a short run of lightweight E-types which are now highly prized.

Above: *The familiar XK engine, a straight-six with twin overhead camshafts, provided the motive power for the E-type. This 3.8-litre engine is fed by three SU carburettors.*

Below: *The Series I fixed-head coupé is perhaps the best looking of all E-types – and surely one of the most admired classic cars of all.*

A better gearbox and a torquier, 4.2-litre engine were introduced in 1964, and a two-plus-two coupé followed in 1966. Nine inches longer than the two-seater and an inch and a half taller, the two-plus-two was oddly proportioned – giving it an ungainly appearance.

Numerous small changes were implemented in what became known as the 'Series One and a Half', including a change to open, sealed beam headlamps, before the Series II proper was unveiled in 1968. The headlamps had been moved forward slightly and bigger indicators fitted, and the air intake had been enlarged to admit cooling air for the new optional air conditioning. Inside rocker switches replaced protruding toggle switches.

By the end of the 1960s increasingly stringent emissions rules in the US meant that a 'Federal' E-type produced just 177bhp. More power was a priority, and it came from a brand new V12 engine designed by Walter Hassan and Harry Mundy. In American specification the V12 offered a genuine 250bhp, despite lacking the fuel injection system originally planned – instead it was fuelled by a quartet of Zenith Stromberg carbs, and sparked by Lucas Opus electronic ignition. The V12 Series III E-type of 1971 used the longer wheelbase of the old two-plus-two car, with flared wheel arches, wider wheels and a new flush grille.

In the US the Huffaker Engineering and Group 44's Bob Tullius built successful racing machines based on Series III E-types, but even so the basic design was being overtaken by more modern rivals. The final E-types were sold in 1975. Jaguar never directly replaced the model, instead introducing a more refined and luxurious GT car, the XJ-S.

Thanks to its stunning looks and still-impressive performance, the E-type is a favourite among classic car enthusiasts the world over.

Above: *The E-type's luscious curves derived from the aerodynamically shaped D-type racing car of the 1950s. The huge, tip-forward bonnet was a complex and expensive structure – and sadly, an easy one to damage through an ill-judged parking manoeuvre.*

1961 Jaguar E-type

Engine 3781cc in-line six

Bore x stroke 87 x 106mm

Valvegear Twin chain-driven overhead camshafts

Fuel system Three SU carburettors

Power 265bhp at 5500rpm

Suspension Front: wishbones, torsion bars, and anti-roll bar; rear: independent with lower wishbone, radius arms, twin coil-spring/damper units and anti-roll bar

Wheels 15in wire wheels

Brakes Hydraulic disc brakes all round, servo assisted

Top speed 149mph (240km/h)

Lincoln Continental

Edsel Ford's Lincoln Continental was phased out in the late 1940s, but the Continental name reappeared as a marque in its own right in 1955. The Continental MkII was a vast, hand-built coupé with a $10,000 asking price, despite which Ford reputedly lost $1000 on each one. The next generation were lower-priced and in 1959 the Continental became a Lincoln again, but remained one of America's biggest and most flamboyant cars.

For 1961 a brand new and very different Continental was offered. Here was proof that less is, indeed, more: the new car was smaller and less ostentatious, with classic clean-cut styling that was the antithesis of the baroque excesses that it replaced. Just two models were available, a four-door saloon and a four-door convertible, both with forward-opening 'suicide' rear doors. A more than adequate 300bhp was provided by a 7.0-litre V8 engine driving the rear wheels through standard automatic transmission. In 1964 a long-wheelbase version was unveiled and in 1966 an even larger 7.6-litre V8 giving 365bhp was installed.

The Continental proved to be just the kind of luxury saloon upmarket buyers wanted in the 1960s, and more than 340,000 were built between 1961 and 1969. For several years the White House used Continentals as official cars – John F Kennedy was assassinated in his – while another appeared as crime boss transport in the film *Goldfinger*. American audiences were horrified when a real Continental (less its engine) was craned into a crusher and cubed…

Above: *The convertible version of the '61 Lincoln Continental was a four-door car, like the saloon. The powered hood folded back effortlessly leaving an uncluttered rear deck.*

Below: *The Continental was one of America's most prestigious cars – so when a real car was crushed in the James Bond film* Goldfinger, *audiences were aghast.*

Mercedes-Benz 300SE/280SE 3.5

The mid-range Mercedes-Benz 'fintail' saloons of 1959 were joined by very elegant four-seater coupés and convertibles in 1961. At first there was just one engine, the fuel-injected 2195cc six with 120bhp, but in 1962 Mercedes-Benz topped off the saloon, coupé and cabriolet ranges with a 2996cc, 170bhp six with a choice of manual or automatic gearboxes. Disc brakes were fitted all round and the cars were equipped with air suspension derived from that in the 600 limousine. These 300SE models were twice the price of the 220SE, so inevitably production was limited.

A new range of W108 saloons appeared in 1965 and the fintail saloons were phased out, but the coupé and cabriolet models remained in production. The new 2496cc seven-bearing straight-six engine from the W108 250SE saloon was fitted from 1965 to 1968, and then the 2778cc 280SE engine took over until 1971. Both cars were fitted with all-disc brakes and the latest development of the Mercedes swing-axle rear suspension, while power assisted steering and an automatic gearbox were options.

The most exciting car in this revised range came in 1969, when Mercedes' new 3.5-litre V8 engine (also used in the long-wheelbase W109 saloon and soon destined for the SL sports car) was fitted to produce the confusingly named 280SE 3.5. With 200bhp on tap, the V8-engined cars were capable of 125mph (201km/h).

Few cars can match the elegance of these 1960s coupés and convertibles, and even fewer can remain unruffled while providing the kind of performance available thanks to the efficient Mercedes straight-six and V8 engines. It's no wonder that these remain some of the most sought-after post-war Mercedes-Benz models of all.

Above: *The Mercedes-Benz coupés and cabriolets of the 1960s had clean, elegant lines with a timeless quality. Potent engines gave them a fair turn of speed, too. This is a 280SE.*

1962 Mercedes-Benz 300SE

Engine 2996cc in-line six

Bore x stroke 85 x 88mm

Valvegear Single overhead camshaft

Fuel system Bosch fuel injection

Power 157bhp at 5000rpm

Suspension Front: double wishbones with air springs and anti-roll bar; rear: swing axles with air springs and anti-roll bar

Wheels 5.5 x 13in steel wheels

Brakes Disc brakes all round

Top speed 109mph (175km/h)

Triumph TR4/5/6

Above: Michelotti created a brand new body for the Triumph TR4 of 1961, but the mechanicals underneath the new model were largely those of the outgoing TR3a.

Triumph's 'sidescreen' TRs proved popular, but by the end of the 1950s their styling was looking old fashioned. Italian stylist Michelotti was contracted to rework the TR3a, and he came up with an attractive full-width body with prominent headlamps. The TR4 carried forward fundamentally the same chassis, with minor improvements such as servo brakes and rack and pinion steering. A 2138cc engine was standard, providing 100bhp, which rose to 104bhp in the TR4a of 1964. More importantly the TR4a gained semi-trailing arm independent rear suspension, which improved the car's ride quality and ensured that it retained grip even on bumpy roads.

In 1967 the four-cylinder engine was replaced by a 2.5-litre straight-six for the 150bhp TR5, the first British car with fuel injection. Sadly the injected engine could not meet stringent American emissions regulations, so the US got twin Stromberg carburettors and a much less exciting output of 104bhp. The triple 'go-faster' stripe across the bonnet was little consolation.

For 1969 Karmann restyled the front and rear (but left the middle of the car alone to minimise re-tooling costs) to produce the TR6, but the chassis and engines remained much the same as before. The fuel injected cars were slightly detuned in 1972 with the fitment of a milder camshaft, but most of the quoted 25bhp power drop was accounted for by a difference in measurement standards. Three quarters of the TR6s produced were US-spec carburettored cars, which continued in production until 1976.

Below: *A fuel-injected straight-six engine gave the TR5 plenty of smooth power. Sadly North American customers had to make do with the much less powerful carburettor-fed TR250.*

Alpine A110

Rally driver Jean Rédélé fitted a Renault 4CV platform with a glassfibre body in 1955, and called the resulting sports car the Alpine A106. He proved the car's potential by winning his class in the Mille Miglia with one, and over the next five years built around 150 examples. The prettier A108 was introduced in 1958, and the shape of the A108 coupé was refined for the most significant Alpine of all, the A110, in 1962.

Like the A108, the new car was built on a steel backbone chassis with a rear-mounted engine and the body was glassfibre. But where the A108 used the 747cc Renault 4CV engine, or later the 845cc Dauphine unit – delivering up to 68bhp in tuned form – the A110 used engines from the Renault R8 and later the Renault 16. Ultimately it had 138bhp at its disposal and coupled with the Alpine's feather weight (just 1500lb/680kg) that meant shattering performance.

The rearward weight bias created by the rear-mounted engine also gave the Alpine excellent traction, which made it a superb car for the loose-surface special stage events which were now taking over from navigational tests in the sport of rallying. In fully developed form it became a regular international rally winner, wrapping up the inaugural world championship for makes in 1973.

Remarkably, despite the A110's clear bias towards competition – it was noisy, and tricky to handle for a road car – more than 8000 were built in a 14-year production run which continued until 1977. Rédélé was always more interested in competition machinery so although a four-seater A110 GT4 was developed in 1963 it was not pursued beyond 1965, and just 112 were built.

Above: *The rear-engined, Renault-based Alpine A110 was a very effective rally car. Light weight and excellent traction were major factors.*

Below: *Workmanlike Alpine cockpit reflected the car's bias towards competition. Despite the lack of creature comforts more than 8000 A110s were sold between 1962 and 1977.*

AC Shelby Cobra

Some cars are created through the vision of a single-minded individual, but the Cobra's genesis was more tortuous. The story began with a twin-tube chassis designed for club racing by John Tojiero and featuring all-independent suspension with a transverse leaf-spring at the rear. In 1952 Cliff Davis had fitted one of these chassis with a 2.0-litre Bristol engine and a very pretty alloy body inspired by a Ferrari 166 Barchetta. The car came to the attention of Charles Hurlock of AC, who bought the car and decided to put it into production. The AC Ace was born, in 1954.

AC fitted its own overhead-cam 2.0-litre engine which gave 85bhp in triple-carburettor form, then offered Bristol engines as an option from 1956. When Bristol moved to Chrysler V8 power, AC looked around for an alternative and settled on tuned 2.6-litre Ford Zephyr engines.

Meanwhile, American race driver and engineer Carroll Shelby had come up with the idea of installing a powerful American V8 engine in a neat-handling European sports car chassis. As a driver Shelby had won at Le Mans for Aston Martin in 1959, and he went to his old team with the idea. Aston Martin showed interest but had other priorities, so Shelby approached AC with backing from Ford's Walter Hayes for supplies of Ford's new V8 engine. In the autumn of 1962 the first Cobra was built, Shelby dropping a 260ci (4261cc) Ford V8 into a mildly revised Ace chassis.

Top and above: *American Ford V8 power turned AC's pretty Ace into the scorching Cobra. Comprehensive instrumentation kept the driver in touch with the engine's health.*

Below: *Serious straight-line performance was a Cobra speciality, but the twin-tube chassis was really overwhelmed by the engine's power. Later cars had a redesigned chassis.*

Above: *Early Cobras lacked the bulbous arches introduced later to cover vast Halibrand alloy wheels and wide tyres. Performance steadily increased as ever larger engines were fitted, culminating in a monstrous 7.0-litre V8 with more than 400bhp.*

The addition of V8 power made the Cobra extraordinarily fast – the sprint from rest to 100mph (161km/h) took just 14 seconds, still a more than respectable figure today. The chassis struggled to cope with the V8 power, but the Cobra was destined to become even more powerful. For 1963 the engine was upgraded to a 4.7-litre (289ci) unit, which could propel this Mk2 Cobra from rest to 60mph (97km/h) in less than six seconds and go on to 138mph (222km/h). The Cobra became a force in sports car racing, as well as an adrenaline-producing road car. At first only available in the US, it went on sale in Britain in right-hand drive form in 1964. That same year special Cobra coupés won the GT category at the Le Mans 24-hour race.

With Ford's help the Cobra chassis was completely redesigned for 1965. The new chassis was wider and stiffer, and it was fitted with more sophisticated coil and wishbone suspension all round (replacing the transverse leaf rear-end inherited from the Ace). Halibrand centre-lock alloy wheels were fitted and the bodywork revised with the addition of bulbous extended arches to cover the fat tyres. Powering this new Cobra was an even larger engine, the famous 427ci (6997cc) V8 which Ford had developed for NASCAR racing and which would power the Mk2 GT40s to victory at Le Mans in 1966. Cobra production continued until 1967, the last few built with the slightly larger but cheaper and less powerful Ford 428ci (7014cc) V8 engine.

The Cobra reappeared in 1983, initially as the 'AC MkIV', but Ford granted permission to use the Cobra name again in 1986. Today a revitalised AC produces MkV cars with modern engines. The Cobra legend continues…

1965 AC Shelby Cobra 427
Engine 6997cc V8
Bore x stroke 107.7 x 96mm
Valvegear Pushrod overhead valve
Fuel system Two Holley carburettors
Power 410bhp at 6000rpm
Suspension Front: wishbones, coil springs; rear: wishbones, coil springs
Wheels Halibrand 15in alloy wheels
Brakes Hydraulic disc brakes all round, servo assisted
Top speed 165mph (266km/h)

Lotus Elan/+2

Key features of the Elan, new in 1962, were the chassis and engine. Unlike the glassfibre monocoque Elite that it replaced, the Elan had an unstressed glassfibre body mounted on a pressed-steel backbone chassis, forked at either end to provide engine and suspension mounting points. Disc brakes and all-round independent suspension – the latter developed with Lotus' usual flair – meant the chassis could cope with plenty of power.

To provide it, Lotus boss Colin Chapman came up with a plan for a new engine to replace the expensive and temperamental Coventry Climax unit in the Elite. Chapman hired Harry Mundy to design a twin-cam conversion for Ford's new Cortina engine, and sold Ford the idea of using the twin-cam powerplant both for his Elan and for a high-performance saloon (which became the Lotus-Cortina). Early engines were 1498cc but most were 1558cc, giving 106bhp from the start and up to 126bhp by the early 1970s.

By then the two-seater Elan – available in hardtop coupé and roadster forms – had been joined by a longer, wider two-plus-two coupé called the Elan +2. Though the +2 wasn't quite as crisp to drive as the two-seater Elan, the extra space was useful and it could still cover the ground quicker than almost anything else.

The Elan continued until 1973, the last of them in big-valve Sprint form with two-tone paint (commonly red over white with gold stripes, Team Lotus' Gold Leaf sponsor colours) and a very few with five-speed gearboxes. The +2 lasted little longer, being replaced by the bigger and faster Elite in 1974.

Above: *Lotus followed the glassfibre monocoque Elite with the Elan, based on a pressed-steel backbone chassis. This is the later Elan +2, which offered two-plus-two accommodation.*

Below: *All the Elans were exceptional driver's cars, with excellent grip and phenomenal balance. Power came from various versions of the Lotus-Ford twin-cam engine.*

MG MGB/MGC

MG's new monocoque sports car for 1962 was another home-grown success for Abingdon. It boasted more power than the outgoing MGA thanks to a bigger (1798cc) three-bearing engine, a higher axle ratio for more refined cruising on Britain's newly-constructed motorways, and front discs in case of emergency. A handsome fastback coupé, called the MGB GT, was added to the range in 1965 bringing with it a five-bearing engine and a quieter axle, which were adopted on the roadster in 1967.

The same year a new six-cylinder engine was squeezed under the bonnet (necessitating a compact new front suspension system with torsion bars) to produce the MGC and MGC GT. The heavy engine made the handling disappointing and it couldn't match the now-defunct Austin-Healey 3000 for performance (though two works MGC racing cars showed some potential) so the C was relatively unsuccessful.

Far better was the MGB GT V8, using the lightweight all-alloy Rover V8 engine. It was fast and handled tidily, but sold in lower numbers than the MGC had done. That rarity makes it a sought-after classic today.

Black polyurethane bumpers were adopted in 1974, along with an increase in ride height, to meet new North American safety requirements, but the handling suffered. Meanwhile power outputs continued to drop on export cars as emissions controls tightened. The MGB soldiered on, with little real development, until 1980.

But that wasn't quite the end of the road for the MGB. It was briefly revived by Rover in 1992 as the MG RV8, which remains rare and collectable.

Top: *Many MGBs are modified to suit owners' tastes: this car has a non-standard wood-rim steering wheel.*

Above and below: *The MGB is one of the world's best-loved sports cars – tough and reliable, easy to work on, stylish and fun to drive. Those who yearn for more performance can choose the six-cylinder MGC or the MGB V8.*

Triumph Spitfire/GT6

Above: *The low bumper of the original Spitfire was raised in 1967 to meet new North American regulations. The nose would be revised again in 1970 to neaten up the appearance.*

Triumph created one of the most popular of all small sports cars in 1962. The Spitfire was based on the chassis of the 1959 Herald saloon, with a curvy two-seater body by Michelotti, an 1147cc twin-carb engine with 63bhp and disc front brakes. Overdrive, wire wheels and a removable hardtop were soon added to the options list, and from 1965 there was a MkII version with more power (now 67bhp) and better trim.

The GT6 – a Spitfire with a fixed, fastback roofline and 2.0-litre straight-six engine – was added to the range in 1966. The following year the MkIII Spitfire was introduced with a higher front bumper to meet new North American requirements. More importantly there was now a 1296cc engine under the bonnet delivering 75bhp, and bigger front brake calipers. The GT6 adopted the new nose and revised rear suspension the following year.

The styling was tidied up by Michelotti for the MkIV Spitfire and MkIII GT6 of 1970, integrating the high-mounted bumper more neatly into the nose and introducing a new one-piece bumper/wings panel. The rear end was also reworked to echo the styling of the new Stag and MkII Triumph 2000. At the same time the gearing was raised and the swing-axle rear suspension revised.

The GT6 was dropped in 1973, while US-market Spitfires received bigger 1493cc engines, and in late 1974 that engine was made available to home-market buyers in the Spitfire 1500. Though the 71bhp power output was less than the MkIII had boasted back in '67 the 1500 was the most numerous of all Spitfires: nearly 96,000 were made before production ended in 1980.

Below: *The Spitfire cleverly used Triumph Herald components to produce a compact, good-value sports car. For two decades it was the arch-enemy of the MG Midget/Austin-Healey Sprite. A GT6 coupé, with a fastback rear end and six-cylinder engine, was available from 1966.*

Chevrolet Corvette Sting Ray

Above: Bill Mitchell's original Corvette Sting Ray was given a controversial split rear window – though it lasted just one season, it's now a sought-after feature.

A new generation Corvette was unveiled for 1963, with a new box-section chassis on a slightly shorter wheelbase and all-independent suspension. The 250bhp, 327ci (5358cc) V8 engine was carried over from the previous generation Corvette. But the biggest news was the new car's outrageous styling, which had clear influences from Chevrolet's 1958 Stingray racing car and the 1959 XP-720 concept car, both styled by Bill Mitchell who had now taken over from Harley Earl as GM's design boss.

The outlandish shape of the Sting Ray – still in glassfibre, as with previous generations – had boldly curved wings with a hint of Jaguar E-type about them, concealed headlamps and dummy air ducts in the front wings. Previous Corvettes had all been roadsters, but the new car was available either as an open two-seater or as a rakish fastback coupé, with a controversial split rear window. Although the split window made for a more dramatic and cohesive shape it lasted only until 1964 when a conventional rear window was substituted, and some early cars were modified to the later style. But today it is the early cars which are more sought-after, and many a later Corvette has been given the early style window…

In 1965 Chevrolet introduced a new all-disc braking system and a 396ci (6489cc) V8 engine, and in 1966 an even more powerful 427ci (6997cc) V8 appeared. The Sting Ray was offered until 1967, and when a new Corvette appeared for '68 it would drop the 'Sting Ray' name – but it would reappear, as one word, for 1969.

1963 Chevrolet Corvette Sting Ray
Engine 5416cc 90-degree V8
Bore x stroke 101.6 x 83.5mm
Valvegear Pushrod-operated overhead valves
Fuel system Rochester fuel injection
Power 360bhp at 6000rpm
Suspension Front: wishbones, coil springs and anti-roll bar; rear: wishbones, driveshaft links and transverse leaf spring
Wheels 15in alloy wheels
Brakes Drum brakes all round, servo assisted
Top speed 150mph (241km/h)

Ford Lotus-Cortina

Lotus boss Colin Chapman came up with the idea of building a new twin-cam engine, then slotting the result into both his own Elan sports car and a new high-performance saloon. That saloon was the Lotus-Cortina.

The twin-cam conversion designed by Harry Mundy, plus a small increase in capacity, boosted the basic Cortina engine from 60bhp to 105bhp. Chapman's attentions to the Cortina included coil springs and A-frame location for the rear axle, wider wheels and a distinctive livery – all the cars were white with a green flash.

Few other cars of the era offered sports-car performance with four-seat saloon accommodation, and the Lotus-Cortina quickly became an enthusiasts' favourite. It was also a spectacularly successful machine for saloon car racing, particularly in the hands of Jim Clark.

But it wasn't perfect. The A-frame locating the rear axle mounted on the differential casing, and the loads it fed into the axle caused the casing to distort, resulting in oil leaks. It wasn't uncommon to see a racing Lotus-Cortina trailing oil smoke from the rear. From 1966 it reverted to the leaf sprung live axle used on the softer Cortina GT to solve the problem.

In 1967 Ford launched a new Cortina. Though there was a twin-cam model (at first called the Cortina Lotus, later Cortina Twin Cam) it was not the drivers' car the previous model had been, and today it's the Mark 1 Lotus-Cortina which enthusiasts still lust after.

Above: *Comprehensive instrumentation and a Lotus three-spoke steering wheel marked out the Lotus-Cortina's interior.*

Below: *All production Lotus-Cortinas were two-door saloons, in white with a green flash. This car is prepared for historic saloon car racing, which is more popular than ever.*

Mercedes-Benz 230SL/250SL/280SL

In 1963 Mercedes-Benz introduced a single car to replace the mass-market 190SL roadster and the fast, expensive 300SL. The 230SL's clean, angular lines were first seen at the Geneva Salon in March 1963. The elegant hard top, which dipped towards the centre, gave the new SL its 'Pagoda roof' nickname.

The new car was based on the running gear of the W110/111 'Fintail' saloons which had been introduced at the end of the 1950s, and the new SL sports car carried over the saloon's double wishbone front and swing axle rear suspension. Though much shorter than the Fintail, the SL kept the wide saloon track front and rear, which helped provide it with excellent roadholding.

The engine was a development of the M127 unit which had already won a reputation for smoothness and flexibility in the Fintail saloons. For the SL, the M127 engine was bored out 2mm to 82mm, increasing the capacity to 2306cc. A new fuel injection system was fitted, and the engine delivered 150bhp at 5500rpm.

The 2.3-litre unit had to be revved hard to make the most of its power. To improve drivability a longer-stroke 2.5-litre engine (the M129) was fitted in 1967, giving the newly-named 250SL no more power than before but considerably more mid-range torque.

The 280SL of 1968 had even more capacity (2778cc) and even more power (now up to 170bhp). It remained in production until 1971, when Mercedes-Benz announced its replacement, the R107 350SL.

Top and above: *A 2.8-litre six-cylinder engine with 170bhp made the 280SL the quickest of the 'Pagoda roof' SLs.*

Below: *Saloon-car comfort and faultless build quality were major attractions of the SLs. Power steering and automatic transmission made them easy to drive.*

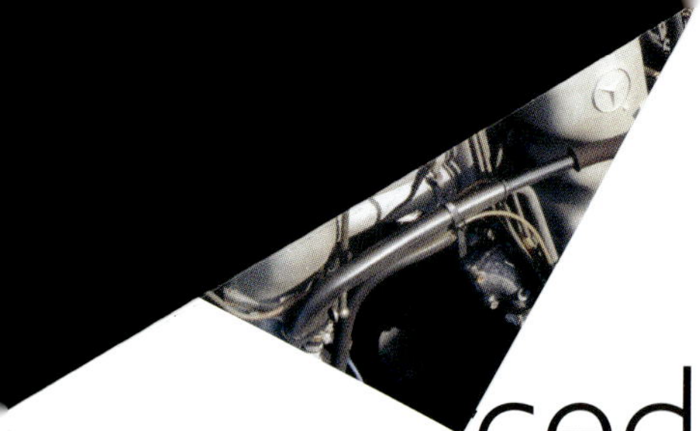

cedes-Benz 600

A serious vehicle for heads of state and captains of industry, offering the last word in luxury and a reasonable turn of speed to get you to your meetings on time. A 6.3-litre, 250bhp V8 (Mercedes-Benz's first) made sure of that by providing a top speed of 127mph (205km/h) and acceleration from rest to 62mph (100km/h) in ten seconds, while automatic transmission, power steering, all-disc brakes and air suspension made for safe and seamless progress.

The 600 was announced at the Frankfurt show in 1963 and production began in September the following year. The standard car was 18ft (5.5m) long and weighed 5500lb (2500kg), but if you needed more space there was also the long-wheelbase Pullman limousine – all of 20ft 5in (6.2m) long and weighing 5850lb (2653kg), with four or six doors and seating up to nine VIPs. The Landaulet, with a fold-down fabric roof at the back of the cabin, was built to special order in very small numbers. A special Landaulet built in September 1965 was used by the Vatican, serving three popes before being returned to Daimler-Benz in 1985. It is now in the company's museum.

Also available to special order were bullet-proof security cars, the first of which was built in 1965 with a special high roofline and which was retained by Daimler-Benz for hire to governments and other organisations. Production bullet-proof 600 limousines were available from 1971.

By the end of the run in June 1981 there had been 2677 600s sold, of which 429 were Pullmans and 59 Landaulets.

Above: *Imposing headlamp units and the familiar Mercedes grille dominate the 600's front end. Despite its size, the big Mercedes could reach 127mph (204km/h).*

Below: *This standard 600 is a roomy machine, but long-wheelbase six-door Pullman limousines offered even more space and comfort. A Landaulet with a fold-down rear roof was also available, but in small numbers.*

Pontiac GTO

Above: *This 1967 GTO starred in the 2002 action movie 'XXX', alongside Vin Diesel and Samuel L. Jackson.*

'Muscle cars' were born in 1964 with the release of the Pontiac Tempest GTO. General Motors had banned its divisions from motor racing, which had been a major part of Pontiac's promotional activities. So instead the focus switched to high-performance road cars. The recipe was simple: take the new Tempest 'intermediate' saloon and drop in a 389ci (6374cc) V8 engine as used in the full-size Pontiac Catalina and Bonneville. Corporate rules dictated that intermediate models could not have engines larger than 330ci (5408cc) but this was to be an option package, not a model in its own right, so it slipped through a loophole…

John Z DeLorean, then Pontiac's chief engineer, came up with the name. 'GTO' was the designation of the fastest of the Ferrari 250 range, and purists were outraged that a mere Pontiac was impertinently appropriating the initials.

The GTO package cost just $300. There was a choice of two specifications for the 389ci (6374cc) V8, either with a four-barrel carb and 325bhp, or three twin-choke carbs and 348bhp. The package also included a twin exhaust system, faster steering and high-performance tyres. Production was initially limited to 5000, but the GTO was a huge success and more than 30,000 were sold. A crisp restyle for 1965 made the GTO even more popular: more than 75,000 were built, most of them hardtop coupés.

From 1966 the GTO was a model in its own right, and it continued to offer bargain-priced performance until emissions regulations began to strangle the powerful V8s in the late 1960s.

1966 Pontiac GTO
Engine 6474cc 90-degree V8
Bore x stroke 103.2 x 95.3mm
Valvegear Pushrod-operated overhead valves
Fuel system Triple Rochester carburettors
Power 360bhp at 5200rpm
Suspension Front: wishbones and coil springs; rear: four-link live rear axle with leaf springs
Wheels 14in steel wheels
Brakes Drum brakes all round, servo assisted
Top speed 120mph (193km/h)

Porsche 911

The early 1960s saw the Porsche 356 nearing the end of its development. The air-cooled flat-four engine had been extended from 1.1 litres to a full 2.0 litres and the bodywork had been enlarged and reshaped to improve passenger space, but Porsche wanted something even bigger and faster. A new car with a new engine was necessary, and it arrived in 1964.

The new design retained the 356's basic layout, mounting an air-cooled, horizontally-opposed engine behind the rear axle line. But the engine was all-new, a 130bhp six-cylinder unit with a single overhead camshaft on each cylinder bank. The suspension, however, was very different: at the front the 356's trailing arms gave way to more compact torsion-sprung struts, and at the rear the tricky swing axles were replaced by semi-trailing arms. The new car was longer so that it could offer more interior space, and was given a distinctive shape by Ferdinand Alexander Porsche.

Porsche called its new machine the 901, until Peugeot objected. The French company had long used three-digit numbers with a central zero for its own cars, so Porsche renamed its new model the 911, and an icon was born.

Early on the 911 proved to be unstable in a straight line, and in corners it generated strong initial understeer and violent lift-off oversteer. And it handled differently in left- and right-hand corners. Some examples were worse than others, and the cause was traced to production variations which upset the suspension geometry. A quick fix was to insert an 24lb (11kg) cast-iron weight

Below: *The 911 took over from the 356 in 1964, offering more interior space and greater performance than its predecessor. It became an iconic sports car.*

Above: *F.A. 'Butzi' Porsche designed the 911's clean and well-proportioned fastback shape. Attractive alloy wheels were a popular option, standard on faster versions.*

Above: *The 911's flat-six engine began at 2.0 litres and was progressively enlarged. Note the large fan at the rear which draws air over the air-cooled engine.*

into each end of the front bumper, to make the weight distribution less rear-biased and to increase the polar moment of inertia, making the 911 stable in corners.

Another problem was a flat spot in the middle of the rev-range. The solution was to ditch the special triple-barrel Solex carbs originally fitted to 911s in favour of triple-choke Weber carbs which had originally been designed for Lancia V6 engines.

Early cars were all fixed-head coupés, but in 1965 Porsche introduced an open-top 911 with a substantial fixed roll-over hoop, a removable roof section and a drop-down rear window (though this was quickly changed to a fixed, wrap-around rear screen). Porsche called it a 'Targa' top, named after the Targa Florio road race which Porsche had already won on four occasions.

A 911S with bigger valves and higher compression appeared in 1967, and then in 1971 the stroke of the flat-six engine was increased to produce a capacity of 2341cc. In 1973 Porsche unveiled probably the most sought after 911 of all, the Carrera RS, with a big-bore 2687cc engine and 210bhp, together with a lightweight body, thinner glass and no rear seats. The combination of greater power and lighter weight made the Carrera RS one of the fastest 911s of the 1970s.

Throughout that decade Porsche would try to replace the 911, notably with the front-engined, water-cooled 928 – but the 911 kept on selling. Regular revisions kept the range fresh, including the addition of a 231bhp 3.2-litre normally-aspirated engine and a full cabriolet.

But time was against the 911. More than a quarter of a century after production began it was comprehensively re-engineered as the type 964.

1972 Porsche 911 Carrera RS
Engine 2687cc air-cooled flat six
Bore x stroke 90 x 70.4mm
Valvegear Single overhead camshaft per cylinder bank
Fuel system Bosch K-Jetronic fuel injection
Power 210bhp at 6300rpm
Suspension Front: struts and torsion bars; rear: semi-trailing arms and torsion bars
Wheels 6 x 15in alloy front wheels, 7 x 15in alloy rear wheels
Brakes Hydraulic disc brakes all round, servo assisted
Top speed 150mph (241km/h)

Studebaker Avanti

Raymond Loewy, the famous industrial designer, was responsible for the Avanti's outlandish shape. In retrospect Loewy's clean-cut design looks like something from the 1970s, but the Avanti went into production in 1962 in an era when Americans were obsessed with excessive chrome trim and unnecessary ornament.

The Avanti's glassfibre body was mounted on a box-section steel chassis with wishbone front suspension and a leaf-sprung live axle at the back. The all-iron V8 engine of 4736cc, either normally aspirated or fitted with a Paxton supercharger, drove through a three-speed manual gearbox, or four-speed manual, or a three-speed Borg-Warner automatic.

Though the Avanti had been conceived as a high-profile sports coupé to help stem the tide of financial trouble which was threatening to engulf Studebaker, it was a lost cause. Production ground to a halt in 1963, and Studebaker moved production of other models from its plant at South Bend, Indiana to Canada. Car production ceased entirely in 1966.

But the Avanti lived on. Studebaker dealers Nathan Altman and Leo Newman bought the rights in July 1964 and built the Avanti II, with modified styling and a 327ci (5359cc), 300bhp Chevrolet Corvette V8 engine. Production continued on a small scale right up to 1985.

The company passed to new owners, who introduced Avanti models with similar styling but based on modern GM platforms in 1986. Avantis are in still in production today in coupé and convertible forms, with a choice of V6 and V8 engines.

Above: *The Avanti's extraordinary shape was by renowned industrial designer Raymond Loewy. The gentle curves and lack of chrome adornment were years ahead of their time.*

Below: *Studebaker put the Avanti into production in 1962, but the company's financial troubles soon intervened. The Avanti was rescued by two of the firm's dealers in 1964, and production continued right through to the 1980s.*

Ferrari 275GTB/GTS

Successor to the famed Ferrari 250 series, the 275 was faster in a straight line and handled better in corners. It also provided Pininfarina with the opportunity to produce one of its best automotive designs, a lithe and aggressive shape with a compact cabin and shark-like nose.

Under the bonnet the new car used an enlarged version of the Colombo V12 that had served the 250 so well. A 77mm bore had already been used in the 4.0-litre 400 Superamerica, and this was mated with the 250's 58.8mm stroke to produce a capacity of 3286cc. In the GTB coupé the V12 delivered 280bhp, while the convertible GTS made do with 'only' 260bhp. To help handle the power the rear suspension was updated from the antiquated live axle of earlier cars to a more modern all-independent system with double wishbones and coil springs. Also new was a five-speed gearbox mounted in unit with the final drive.

A Series II with a longer nose and reshaped bonnet appeared in 1965, but the following year the big news was *under* the bonnet. The valvegear of the V12 was revised with twin overhead camshafts on each cylinder bank, boosting power to 300bhp at 8000rpm, and the car became known as the 275GTB/4 to denote its four camshafts. Just a handful of four-cam cars were built as convertibles, all of them for the American market.

The 275GTB/4 continued in production until 1968, when it was replaced by another classic Pininfarina-styled Ferrari, the 365GTB/4 'Daytona'. But thanks to their rarity the two-cam and four-cam 275GTBs are worth more in today's market.

Above: *The 275GTB benefited from one of Pininfarina's best styling efforts, a tight and tense shape hinting at the power within. Early cars had two-cam V12 engines with 280bhp, later ones four cams and 300bhp.*

1963 Ferrari 275GTB/4

Engine 3286cc 60-degree V12

Bore x stroke 77.0 x 58.8mm

Valvegear Twin overhead camshafts per cylinder bank

Fuel system Six Weber carburettors

Power 300bhp at 8000rpm

Suspension Front: double wishbones, coil springs and anti-roll bar; rear: double wishbones and coil springs

Wheels 15in alloy wheels

Brakes Disc brakes all round, servo assisted

Top speed 168mph (270km/h)

Ford Mustang

Lee Iacocca's 'pony car' took America by storm in 1964. It was the right car at the right time – an attractive, sporty two-door available in a variety of body styles, with a choice of different engines, a long list of options and a tempting basic price.

The Mustang slotted into a market sector which had been vacated by Ford as the Thunderbird grew up into a much larger, heavier machine than the '55 original. The gap was filled by a compact machine (though a four-seater, unlike the two-seat T-bird) which drew heavily on the mechanical components of the Falcon. That meant conventional semi-elliptic leaf springs and a live rear axle at the back, and drum brakes as standard with front discs as an option.

The engine choice encompassed everything from a 101bhp, 2.8-litre straight six to a 4.7-litre V8 delivering 271bhp. It wasn't long before tuners were queuing up to give the Mustang more power, and Carroll Shelby's GT-350 offered muscle-car pace and race-track competitiveness.

But the Mustang's real success was in the showroom: more than 400,000 were sold in the first year, many with profit-winning options from the extensive list of extras. Ford did little to alter its winning formula until the Mustang was restyled in 1968. 'Big block' V8 engines offered still greater power outputs but the Mustang was increasing in size and weight, as the Thunderbird had done. By the 1970s insurance worries and fuel crises had turned the focus back to small, efficient cars – and the smaller, slower 2.3-litre Mustang II had taken over.

Above and below: *Ford hit the right spot with the Mustang, a compact and sporty car available in several different body styles, with a variety of engines and with a long list of options allowing plenty of personalisation.*

Marcos

Jem Marsh and Frank Costin – from whose truncated surnames the name derives – built the first Marcos GT in 1960. Strictly speaking it had composite monocoque construction, the composite in this case being nothing less than marine plywood. It was hideously ugly, but Jackie Stewart and others proved its effectiveness on the race track.

In 1964 Marcos moved on to the Dennis Adams-designed GT with a tightly-drawn glassfibre body over a plywood chassis, initially powered by a Volvo 1.8-litre in-line four and later using Ford engines with up to 120bhp. De Dion rear suspension was fitted at first, but after about 50 were built the GT was give a coil-sprung live axle.

The Mini-Marcos, a glassfibre monocoque coupé using Mini mechanicals, was introduced in 1965 to run alongside the GT, which adopted Ford's new 3.0-litre 'Essex' V6 in 1968. The wooden chassis was phased out in favour of a steel item. For export Marcos also fitted a 130bhp straight-six Volvo engine, and a few cars were sold with the 2.5-litre Triumph six. A 2.0-litre Ford V4 was fitted to the final cars built before the company failed in 1971, not aided by an ill-conceived four-seater, the spaceframe Mantis.

Jem Marsh continued to offer parts and service for Marcos cars until 1981, when production was restarted. In 1984 the Rover V8-engined Mantara was unveiled and two years later a convertible, the Mantula, was added to the range.

A revitalised Marcos, under new boss Tony Stelliga, now produces the TVR-baiting TSO cars with American GM V8 power units.

Above: *Despite its low nose the Marcos is a front-engined car. This is the 1800, powered by a 1.8-litre in-line four from Volvo. Ford and Volvo 3.0-litre engines were later available in the same body.*

Below: *Rear view emphasises the low build of the Marcos. The body is glassfibre, while the chassis of early cars was fabricated from plywood. A steel chassis took over later.*

Ford GT40

Ford wanted a flagship performance brand. Ferrari wanted the financial security a major automotive industry partner could give it. Discussions between Ford and Ferrari about a takeover continued for some time in the early 1960s until, at the last minute, Enzo Ferrari said no.

Henry Ford II resolved to beat Ferrari at his own game, and that meant in competition. The basis of just the car to do just that had already been created in England by Eric Broadley's tiny Lola racing car concern: Ford bought the Lola GT project, and Broadley's services, and recreated it as the Ford GT40 – so called because it was just 40in tall.

Early GT40s were unstable at speed due to aerodynamic effects which were not fully understood at the time. Painstaking development eventually turned the cars into effective racing machines, but not until Ford had spent much time and even more money. Initially GT40s were powered by a 4.7-litre V8 but it was the mighty 7.0-litre Mark 2 version developed by Shelby American which got the job done. Chris Amon and Bruce McLaren brought their Mark 2 home first at Le Mans in 1966, with sister Mark 2s second and third, leaving Ferrari well beaten.

Opposite and above: *Ford's GT40 was built to beat Ferrari in sports car racing – and it achieved its aim at Le Mans in 1966. This is the GT40 Mark 3 road car, which sold in small numbers in the late 1960s.*

Above: *Ducts on top of the nose allow hot air from the front-mounted radiator to escape. The GT40s, which were based on a Lola design, were built in the UK by Ford Advanced Vehicles in Slough, Berkshire.*

GT40 derivatives would go on to win Le Mans in the following three years. The J-type Mark 4 car which won in 1967 in the hands of A.J. Foyt and Dan Gurney used the mechanicals of the Mark 2 in a very different body, but changes in the regulations would make the GT40-proper competitive again. Remarkably both the 1968 and 1969 Le Mans races were won by the same car, GT40 chassis 1075, the second time beating Hans Herrmann's Porsche in a nail-biting close finish.

Ford Advanced Vehicles in Slough, England built 31 GT40 road cars in addition to the racing machines, before launching a true road-going version, the Mark 3, in 1967. Mark 3s were given reworked styling, with four round headlamps and an extended tail to provide luggage space. Inside the trim was more luxurious than in the spartan GT40 race cars and there were wider, adjustable seats in place of the competition GT40's fixed-back chairs. A more significant change was the adoption of a central gearshift in place of the right-hand shift of the race cars, allowing the Mark 3 to be produced in both left- and right-hand drive.

By the 1980s GT40 prices had rocketed to such a degree that a market for replicas was created. Quality varied but some, like the GTD40, were outstanding cars. Ford even sanctioned a Mark 5 GT40 built by Safir Engineering using some original jigs and patterns.

The GT40's significance in Ford history is underlined by Ford's own recreation, the Ford GT, at the turn of the 21st century. But in the eyes of many enthusiasts, there's nothing quite like the real thing.

1966 Ford GT40 MkII

Engine 6997cc V8

Bore x stroke 107.5 x 96.1mm

Valvegear Pushrod overhead valve

Fuel system Four-barrel Holley carburettor

Power 485bhp at 6200rpm

Suspension Front: double wishbones, coil springs and anti-roll bar; rear: trailing arms, lower wishbone, upper transverse link, coil springs and anti-roll bar

Wheels Front: 8 x 15in alloy, rear: 9.5 x 15in alloy

Brakes Hydraulic disc brakes all round

Top speed 203mph (327km/h)

Plymouth Barracuda

The Ford Mustang was by far the more successful, but the Plymouth Barracuda was the first of the 'pony cars', beating the Ford into the marketplace by a couple of weeks.

It started out as the Valiant Barracuda, a fastback coupé option for the Valiant saloon, complete with a vast wrap-around rear window said at the time to be the biggest single piece of glass ever used in a car. Under it was a handy fold-down rear seat. Up front you had the same choice of engines as in the saloons, from a weedy 170ci (2786cc) 'Slant Six' to a punchier 273ci (4477cc) V8 with 235bhp.

The Barracuda only became a true performance car in 1967, when the Slant Six was dropped and three V8s were offered – two versions of the 273, and a 383ci (6276cc) behemoth so big there was no room for a power steering pump. The unassisted steering made it hard work to drive. Plymouth shoe-horned the power steering pump into the engine bay for 1969, but then raised the game again with an even bigger 440ci (7210cc) V8 which came with unassisted steering and automatic transmission only.

A new Barracuda body arrived for 1970, shared with the Dodge Challenger. Top engine options were the 440 V8 (now available with triple carburettors and 390bhp) and the famous 426 Hemi with 425bhp.

But US emissions laws were tightening, and the big V8s were dropped for 1972, leaving the Barracuda (along with many other muscle cars) a shadow of its former self, though it rumbled on into 1974.

Above: *Plymouth's Barracuda 'pony car' beat the Mustang to the market by a few weeks. The fastback body with its huge rear window was available until 1970.*

Below: *Powerful V8s turned the Barracuda into a real performance car in 1967, but like many muscle cars it was gradually strangled by increasing concerns over emissions and insurance premiums in the early 1970s.*

Buick Riviera

Buick introduced the flagship Riviera luxury coupé for the 1963 season. Its engineering was Detroit conventional, with a separate chassis, drum brakes and a choice of V8 engines – a 401ci (6571cc) V8 and a choice of two 425ci (6965cc) engines, offering 340bhp or (with two four-barrel carbs) 360bhp and top speeds of up to 125mph (201km/h).

But it was not the Riviera's performance which was its major appeal, but its styling. Conceived by GM chief designer Bill Mitchell (also responsible for the controversial and now very sought-after 'split window' Corvette Sting Ray) the Riviera was a handsome two-door hardtop with frameless side windows and clean lines which broke away from the baroque excesses perpetrated elsewhere in the US auto industry.

The 1965 model was the ultimate expression of the first generation Riviera, with hidden headlamps in the front wings and full-width tail lights. A 'Gran Sport' option was now offered which combined the more potent of the two 425ci V8s with a Posi-Traction limited-slip differential and shorter gearing.

A second-generation Riviera was unveiled for 1966 and still proved popular, though the shape lacked the character of the earlier car. A third-generation car introduced in 1970 had 'boat tail' styling which recaptured some of the Riviera's original appeal, but as with other American performance cars of the time, tightening emissions laws strangled the output of the V8 engines. The Riviera name would continue into the 1990s, but none of the cars would be nearly as memorable as the classic Rivieras of the early 1960s.

Above: *Sweeping lines gave the Riviera its appeal. The styling was credited to Bill Mitchell, GM's chief designer, who was also responsible for the Corvette Sting Ray.*

Below: *Typical Detroit comforts abound inside the Riviera, which was positioned as Buick's flagship model. This 1963 model is one of the first-generation Rivieras, but the name lived on right into the 1990s.*

Iso Grifo

Above: *Iso was an Italian company and the Grifo's aggressive styling was by Bertone, but the motive power came from a Chevrolet V8 engine, first a 5.3-litre unit and later a 7.0-litre.*

Renzo Rivolta's Iso company moved on from refrigerators and air conditioning to motorcycles and the Isetta bubble car, and then turned to V8-powered GT cars with the two-plus-two Iso Rivolta in 1962. The Grifo two-seater followed in 1963.

Clothed in rakish steel bodywork styled by Giorgetto Giugiaro at Bertone, the Grifo was based on a short-wheelbase version of the Rivolta platform developed by Giotto Bizzarrini. It was powered by a 'solid lifter' Chevrolet Corvette V8 of 5359cc (optional on the Rivolta) which delivered 360bhp. A four-speed manual gearbox was standard but, like the Rivolta, the Grifo could be specified with a five-speed manual or a two-speed automatic. The suspension was independent by wishbones and coil springs at the front, with a De Dion at the rear. Dunlop disc brakes were fitted all round.

An alloy-bodied competition version was also available, the change of bodywork material reducing the Grifo's overall weight by no less than 660lb (300kg). Grifos finished 14th at Le Mans in 1964 and a creditable ninth in 1965. But that year Bizzarrini parted company with Iso, and went on to produce a new version of the Grifo under his own name, as the 5300GT.

In 1968 the Grifo's performance jumped to true supercar levels with the introduction of a 7.0-litre V8 engine offering a generous 435bhp.The extra power raised the Grifo's top speed to 170mph, (274km/h) making it one of the fastest cars of the 1960s.

Marcello Gandini penned an excellent restyle for the front end in 1970, then in 1972 Iso switched to Ford engines. Production ended with Iso's collapse in 1974.

1968 Iso Grifo 7.0-litre
Engine 6992cc 90-degree V8
Bore x stroke 108.0 x 95.5mm
Valvegear Pushrod-operated overhead valve
Fuel system Single Rochester carburettor
Power 390bhp at 5200rpm
Suspension Front: wishbones and coil springs; rear: de Dion with coil springs, transverse links and radius arms
Wheels 15in alloy wheels
Brakes Disc brakes all round, servo assisted
Top speed 171mph (275km/h)

Below: *Giugiaro styled the Grifo while he was working for Bertone, and later the front end was restyled by Marcello Gandini. The Grifo is one of the most handsome shapes of the 1960s.*

Lancia Fulvia

Lancia's first front-wheel drive car was the Flavia of 1960, a boxy saloon with a flat-four engine which plugged the gap between the compact Appia saloon and the limo-like Flaminia. The 1963 Fulvia Berlina saloon was another front-wheel drive car, the replacement for the Appia. It echoed the upright Flavia shape and offered such refinements as all-disc brakes, transverse-leaf independent front suspension, an all-synchro four-speed manual gearbox and Lancia's favourite engine configuration, a narrow-angle V4.

A handsome short-wheelbase Fulvia Coupé styled in-house by Pietro Castagnero appeared in 1965, and was developed into an effective tool for rallying. It won the World Rally Championship in 1972 and 1974, and the European Championship in 1973.

The high-performance road version of the coupé was the HF, with suspension tweaks, tuned engines (eventually with 1584cc and up to 132bhp) and except on HF Lusso models, alloy panels and plastic windows. Fulvia Coupés for the UK market had a distinctive 'raised eyebrow' front end with higher outer headlamps to meet local regulations. A Zagato-bodied fastback coupé was also available from 1967 to 1972, with lightweight alloy bodywork and a rounded nose with rectangular headlamps.

The Fulvia saloon was phased out in 1972, though it would not be truly replaced until the Delta hatchback arrived in 1979, but the Fulvia Coupé continued in 1298cc form. Following Fiat's takeover of Lancia in 1970 and the introduction of Fiat-based Beta models, the Fulvia Coupé became the last remaining 'real' Lancia until its demise in 1976.

Above and below: *In coupé form the Fulvia was both attractive and effective, taking Lancia to numerous rally wins. Note the raised outer headlamps on this early 1970s car, fitted to meet UK regulations on headlamp heights.*

Rolls-Royce Silver Shadow

Modern Rolls-Royces started here. Crewe's staple product from 1965 was a crisply-styled four-door saloon with a monocoque steel body, while two-door saloons were available from coachbuilders James Young and Mulliner Park Ward, the latter with a kink in the rear wings behind the B-post.

Behind the famous radiator grille surmounted as ever by the Spirit of Ecstacy mascot (or the rounded Bentley radiator with a winged 'B') sat the established 6230cc V8 with 'sufficient' power, probably about 200bhp. Power steering, automatic transmission, self-levelling rear suspension and all-round disc brakes were standard.

A two-door convertible arrived in 1967, in 1971 joining the two-door hardtop under the name Corniche. A 4in longer wheelbase was offered in 1968 to add extra rear legroom, all the long wheelbase cars also getting an Everflex vinyl roof covering. A bigger, 6750cc engine arrived in 1970. Flared arches accommodating wider tyres were brought in for 1974. In 1975 Rolls-Royce introduced the Shadow-based Camargue coupé with controversial Pininfarina styling.

In 1977 numerous revisions were incorporated into the Silver Shadow II and long-wheelbase Silver Wraith, including an air dam under the nose, a new fascia, rack and pinion steering and split-level air conditioning. The Shadow and Wraith continued until 1980, when they were replaced by the Silver Spirit and Spur. The Corniches survived much longer, with revised Spirit rear suspension from 1979. Bentley versions adopted the name Continental in 1984, and the cars finally bowed out in 1994.

1965 Rolls-Royce Silver Shadow
Engine 6230cc 90-degree V8
Bore x stroke 104.4 x 91.4mm
Valvegear Pushrod-operated overhead valve
Fuel system Two SU carburettors
Power Not quoted; 200bhp estimated
Suspension Front: wishbones, coil springs and anti-roll bar; rear: semi-trailing arms and coil springs
Wheels 15in steel wheels
Brakes Disc brakes all round, servo assisted
Top speed 120mph (193km/h)

Below: *Sumptuous leather and fine walnut dominate the Silver Shadow interior. Automatic transmission, with a column-mounted selector lever, was standard.*

Left: *As ever the imposing Rolls-Royce radiator grille was topped with the famous 'Spirit of Ecstasy' mascot.*

Alfa Romeo Giulia Sprint GT/GTV

With the advent of a new range of Giulia saloons in 1962, a new range of coupés was sure to follow. They came in 1963, crisply styled by Giorgetto Giugiaro at Bertone and powered by the latest versions of the ubiquitous Alfa twin-cam engine.

The Giulia Sprint GT, with 1570cc and 106bhp, was the first of the line, followed by a GTC four-seater convertible and a slightly more potent GT Veloce or GTV. A lightweight racing version, the GTA, proved extremely successful in European touring car racing while Zagato's lightweight 'Tubolare' versions regularly turned in giant-killing performances in sports car events.

The next major changes came with the introduction of a 1290cc GT Junior and the adoption of a long-stroke 1779cc engine for what was now called the 1750GTV, distinguished externally by its four-headlamp nose.

The Alfa twin-cam was enlarged once again in 1971, this time to 1962cc for the 132bhp 2000GTV which was instantly recognisable by its bright grille bars with raised sections picking out the shape of a traditional Alfa grille.

From the original Giulia Sprint GT to the last of the 2000GTVs, built in 1976, these are some of the best-loved of all the classic Alfas. As beautifully balanced in their road manners as they are in their looks, and yet still reasonably priced and easy to live with, they are among the best value classics of all.

Above: *The neat styling of Alfa Romeo's new generation of coupés was another product of Giorgetto Giugiaro at Bertone.*

Below: *The Giulia coupés were available with various versions of the Alfa twin-cam engine. This is the 1290cc GT Junior.*

Alfa Romeo Duetto/Spider

Hot on the heels of the Alfa Giulia saloon and Sprint coupé came a drophead member of the family, the Duetto, a replacement for the old 101-series Giulia Spider. Opinion was divided about the merits of the Pininfarina-styled boat-tail body with its scalloped sides, particularly after its achingly pretty predecessor, but the Duetto had plenty going for it. The usual Alfa twin cam engine and well-located suspension made it swift, surefooted and fun to drive. The Duetto was given an early boost with a central role in the film *The Graduate*, alongside Dustin Hoffman.

In 1968 the Duetto name was dropped and the 1779cc twin cam adopted: the car was now called the 1750 Spider Veloce. Later that year a 1.3-litre Spider Junior was added to the range. Further changes came in 1970 with a restyled rear end with a vertical tail, and then the adoption of a 1962cc, 131bhp twin cam engine in 1971.

Right-hand drive production stopped in 1977, but the Spider continued to sell in Europe and the USA. Energy absorbing bumpers were added to conform with new legislation, and a flexible plastic spoiler appeared at the back, which both served to obscure the original Pininfarina shape which had otherwise worn well over time. A proper redesign in 1990 gave the Spider neatly contoured, body-coloured bumpers front and rear. Remarkably, the Spider returned to the UK in right-hand drive form in 1991, though by then it was showing its age when compared with modern rivals. Production finally ended in 1994.

Above: *The Duetto and Spider both had comfortable cockpits. It was possible to raise the folding roof from the driver's seat.*

Below: *A reshaped tail with a vertical rear panel came in 1970. Opinions are still divided about which style is better.*

Fiat Dino

Fiat and Ferrari collaborated on a 2.0-litre V6 engine which Ferrari intended to use in Formula 2 racing. To be eligible it had to be built in some numbers, so it was proposed that Ferrari build a new small sports car and Fiat a sporting touring car, all of which would be sold under the Dino name.

In the event the Fiat was badged as the Fiat Dino, and it arrived in 1966. It effectively replaced the 2300S coupé, and like that car it was a steel monocoque car with a live rear axle carried on leaf springs. The curvaceous styling was by Pininfarina, and had hints of the Dino 206GT sports car that Pininfarina had designed for Ferrari and which shared the same 2.0-litre alloy-block V6.

In 1967 a fixed-head coupé, with clean-cut lines by Bertone, was added to the line-up. Revisions to both models came in 1969, when they adopted the latest 2.4-litre version of the 65-degree V6 engine, now with an iron block with wider bores and a longer stroke. Power was up from 165bhp to 180bhp. To cope with the extra torque of the new engine a strong ZF gearbox replaced the Fiat unit of the earlier car, while the live axle was replaced with an independent suspension system with coil springs and semi-trailing arms, similar to the setup used on the Fiat 130 saloon and the 130 coupé which followed a couple of years later.

Dino production continued until 1971. Often overlooked, they make characterful and sensible classic buys today.

Above: *The Fiat Dino is an elegant and characterful machine which today many buyers wrongly ignore. This is the Bertone-styled coupé, built on a longer wheelbase than the curvier Pininfarina-styled roadster.*

1969 Fiat Dino 2.4

Engine 2418cc 65-degree V6

Bore x stroke 92.5 x 60.0mm

Valvegear Twin overhead camshafts per cylinder bank

Fuel system Triple Weber carburettors

Power 180bhp at 6600rpm

Suspension Front: wishbones and coil springs; rear: semi-trailing arms and coil springs

Wheels 15in alloy wheels

Brakes Disc brakes all round, servo assisted

Top speed 130mph (209km/h)

Honda S800

Motorcycle manufacturer Honda turned its attention to cars in 1963 with the S500 sports car, a tiny convertible or coupé powered by a 531cc in-line four. The engine featured a motorcycle-style roller-bearing crankshaft and twin overhead cams, and it delivered 44bhp at a heady 8000rpm through chain drive to the rear wheels.

In 1964, the year Honda went into Formula 1 Grand Prix racing with the V12-engined RA271, it bored and stroked its road-going sports car's engine to increase its capacity to 606cc and boost the power output to 57bhp for the S600. In 1966 still larger bore and stroke dimensions turned the engine into a 791cc unit developing 70bhp not far from the 8500rpm red line, allegedly turning the S800 into a 100mph (161km/h) car. This was the first of the series to be available in the UK.

Neat though unexceptional styling characterised the steel body covering a conventional separate chassis. At the front there was independent suspension by wishbones and torsion bars, while the earlier cars' chain drive and independent rear suspension soon gave way to a live axle comprehensively located by coil springs, a Panhard rod, and radius arms. Disc front brakes were provided, but thanks to the Honda's light weight no servo was necessary.

Though the S800 never achieved the kind of sales success enjoyed by the British roadsters which were its biggest rivals – the Austin-Healey Sprite, MG Midget and Triumph Spitfire – it managed to sell more than 11,000 before production ended in 1971. As a classic it makes a characterful and unusual alternative to the more common small sports cars.

Top: *Honda employed its motorcycle engine know-how in the S800's tiny in-line four.*

Above: *An attractive S800 coupé was available alongside the roadster.*

Below: *The roadster was an interesting, if unconventional, alternative to the Midget, Sprite and Spitfire.*

Jensen Interceptor/FF

Controversial styling didn't help sales of Jensen's fast and luxurious CV8 in the early 1960s. The Interceptor of 1966 offered much the same mechanical package, with a 6.3-litre Chrysler V8 engine and disc brakes, but with a devilishly handsome steel body (the CV8 was glassfibre) styled by Touring and at first built by Vignale in Italy.

The Interceptor was well specified, with servo-assisted disc brakes all round, a Powr-Lok limited-slip differential and automatic transmission (though a manual gearbox was an option at first). In 1969 power-assisted steering became standard equipment. That same year Jensen introduced a new version of the Interceptor, the FF, which incorporated Ferguson Formula four-wheel-drive and the Dunlop Maxaret anti-lock braking system which had originally been designed for aircraft. The combination made the FF exceptionally able in bad weather conditions. The FF's wheelbase was 4in (10cm) longer to incorporate all the extra hardware, and could be identified by the twin (instead of single) cooling vents behind the front wheels.

The styling of both the Interceptor and FF was tidied up in 1970 and 1972 brought ventilated discs, alloy wheels and new rear seats but by then the FF was no more. Despite its extraordinary ability on the road the FF failed to sell because of its high price and similarity in appearance to the standard Interceptor. It was 10 years ahead of its time.

Convertible Interceptors arrived in 1975 and a notchback coupé came in 1975, but Jensen was hit hard by the oil crisis in the early 1970s and the cost of complying with US emissions and safety legislation. Interceptor production ended in 1976, and a revival in the 1980s proved to be brief.

Above: *Jensen's handsome Interceptor offered Italian style and British quality with American grunt – power came from a 6.3-litre Chrysler V8.*

Below: *Vast wrap-around rear window was a characteristic feature of the Interceptor and FF.*

Lamborghini Miura

Ferruccio Lamborghini made his fortune building tractors, then started making his own sports car in 1962, designed by ex-Ferrari engineers Giotto Bizzarrini (responsible for the V12 engine), Giampaolo Dallara and Giampaolo Stanzani (who created the chassis). A new factory was built at Sant'Agata, just outside Bologna, and by 1964 production of the 350GT was in full swing. It was soon followed by the 4.0-litre 400GT and a succession of prototypes and show cars, the wildest of them using a monocoque built up from sheet steel, with a V12 engine mounted transversely behind the cockpit. It was a flight of fancy by the engineering team, inspired by the then-new Ford GT40 racing car.

The chassis made its first public appearance at the Turin show in 1965, where pundits queued up to opine that Lamborghini would never put it into production. But they were wrong: Lamborghini had decided to build the new car as a publicity tool, and barely four months later, in the Spring of 1966, Sant'Agata unveiled a production-ready version. It now had an eye-catching body designed by Bertone's new styling chief, Marcello Gandini, and had acquired the name Miura, after the famous Spanish breeder of fighting bulls, Don Antonio Miura.

Technically, it was very advanced. Its mid-engined layout was the state of the art in sports car racing, and like the 350GT and 400GT before it, the Miura had all-

Above: *Room for two only in the cramped Miura cabin, looking out over the heavily cowled instruments and vented bonnet.*

Below: *Few expected Lamborghini to build production versions of such a wild machine but build them it did, from 1966.*

independent suspension (at a time when some Ferraris still used live axles). Bizzarrini's 3929cc four-cam V12, developing a claimed 350bhp, was fitted in a unit with its transmission and sharing a single oil system (just like the very different BMC Mini). The Miura was beautiful, advanced, and there was no doubt it was fast – the true top speed being over 170mph (274km/h).

A Miura roadster prototype was displayed at the Brussels show in 1968, but never made it into production. Instead Lamborghini introduced a revised Miura S that same year, with many detail improvements under the skin and a claimed 20bhp extra power.

Even more powerful was the Jota, a 440bhp racing Miura prototype developed by New Zealander Bob Wallace. Thanks to the powerful V12 and a lightweight chassis (reducing the Jota's kerb weight to just 1962lb/890kg) the Jota was capable of sprinting from rest to 60mph (97km/h) in less than four seconds. But the car's performance was to hasten its demise. The Jota was sold on by the factory, and shortly after it was completely destroyed in a crash in Brescia.

The idea of a faster Miura lived on in the Miura SV of 1971, which incorporated many of the lessons learned from the Jota. The chassis was built from heavier-gauge steel, the suspension geometry was revised and wider tyres fitted, and there were now individual oil systems for the engine and the gearbox. Power rose to 385bhp, making the SV the fastest of the Miuras as well as the strongest and the best-handling. A handful of SVs were given some of the more extreme Jota modifications by the factory, and were known as SVJs.

1971 Lamborghini Miura SV

Engine 3929cc in-line six

Bore x stroke 82 x 62mm

Valvegear Twin chain-driven overhead camshafts per cylinder bank

Fuel system Four Weber carburettors

Power 385bhp at 7850rpm

Suspension Front: wishbones, coil springs and anti-roll bar; rear: wishbones, coil springs and anti-roll bar

Wheels 15in magnesium alloy wheels

Brakes Hydraulic disc brakes all round, servo assisted

Top speed 170mph (274km/h)

Below: *Lamborghini's V12 engine sat transversely under the slatted rear deck, sharing its oil supply with the gearbox on early cars. The Miura was low, dramatic and very, very fast.*

Maserati Ghibli

Maserati's answer to the Ferrari 275GTB and Daytona was the 170mph (274km/h) Ghibli, introduced in 1966. Giorgetto Giugiaro, then working for Ghia, was responsible for the fantastic shape, with pop-up headlamps inset into a tapering nose and raked-back screen leading into a fastback rear end.

The Ghibli's mechanical configuration could be traced back to the four-door Quattroporte saloon of 1963 and the shorter-wheelbase Mexico coupé derived from it. The Quattroporte had debuted with De Dion rear suspension but the Mexico reverted to a live rear axle on semi-elliptic leaf springs, and the four-door car followed soon after: the same layout was adopted on the Ghibli. Better news was the adoption of disc brakes all round and a choice of five-speed manual gearbox or an automatic transmission.

Maserati's quad-cam V8 engine provided the motive power. Early cars came with a 4.7-litre, 330bhp engine, but in 1970 a Ghibli SS was introduced with a torquier 4.9-litre motor (though maximum power climbed only fractionally).

A gorgeous Ghibli Spider convertible was available from 1969, and could be had with a factory hardtop for all-weather versatility. Coupés outnumber spiders 10 to one so it is rarity as much as glamour which pushes the Spider's prices way beyond those of its fastback cousin, but all Ghiblis come at bargain prices viewed against comparable Ferraris.

Ghibli production ended in 1973, by which time the Italian supercar marques had firmly embraced the mid-engined configuration for their flagship two-seaters – and by then Maserati's first mid-engined car, the Bora, was already on sale.

Top and above: *Awesome Ghibli is another car from the prolific pen of Giorgetto Giugiaro. Inside the swathes of leather, the steering wheel with drilled aluminium spokes and the well-stocked dash are typically 1960s.*

Below: *Ghibli's clean and uncluttered shape hints at its top speed capability: it could achieve more than 170mph (274km/h), making it one of the fastest cars of its era.*

Oldsmobile Toronado

Only in America. What other country would have produced a 17ft 7in (5.4m) car with an all-up weight of 4400lb (1996kg), 385bhp from a 7.0-litre V8, drum brakes – and front-wheel drive? In size, weight and power the Toronado might have been a match for its contemporaries, but in other areas it was a complete departure from Detroit's usual machinery.

The swooping two-door styling with its distinctive flat-faced extensions on each wheel arch was penned under the eye of GM chief stylist Bill Mitchell. It was individual and stylish, although some reviewers complained about poor three-quarter rear vision, the difficulty of judging the car's width and the eight-second delay in raising the pop-up headlamps.

At first the Toronado was powered by a 6965cc V8 driving a three-speed Hydramatic automatic gearbox through a Hy-Vo chain, a mechanical layout also adopted by GM's Cadillac Eldorado in 1967. As if that wasn't enough the 1968 model year Toronados adopted an even larger 7457cc engine with 400bhp, and from 1970 front discs replaced the fade-prone drums to cope with the car's weight and performance.

Revisions to the styling for 1968 gave the nose a split front grille and there were further changes in 1970 when the idea of concealed headlamps was dropped and instead the lamps were inset into the grille.

For 1971 a brand new Toronado appeared, still front-wheel drive but a larger and much less distinctive car than Bill Mitchell's classic original.

Above: *Toronado was a bizarre combination – a big and heavy car in the American tradition, with 7.0 litres and 385bhp, but driving through the front wheels.*

Below: *The Toronado was another car with innovative styling produced under the direction of GM styling chief Bill Mitchell.*

Chevrolet Camaro

The runaway success of Ford's Mustang prompted General Motors to respond with 'pony cars' of its own, and Chevrolet's contribution was the Camaro of 1967. The Camaro coupés and convertibles shared their platform with the new Chevy Nova which would debut the following year. The Camaro's basic structure was a unitary bodyshell, but the engine and suspension were carried by a separate steel subframe.

Early interest surrounded the luxury RS (Rally Sport) and rapid SS (Super Sport) packages, the latter with a 350ci (5736cc) V8 as standard and eventually a 375bhp, 396ci (6489cc) V8 was offered. Late in 1966 another engine was made available, the famous Z-28 small-block V8 – a short-stroke 302ci (4949cc) unit with more than 360bhp which was created for Trans-Am racing, and was never actively promoted as a road-going option.

In 1969 revisions to the styling freshened up the Camaro's looks, with a new inset grille and a horizontal crease along each side. Another powerful engine option was unleashed – the ZL1 included a big-block 427ci (6997cc) V8 with an aluminium block and cylinder heads, delivering something in the region of 500bhp. But the ZL1 was hugely expensive – twice the price of a regular Camaro – and Chevrolet built few more than the 50 needed to make the car legal for NHRA Super Stock drag racing.

A brand new Camaro was unveiled in 1970, and would run through the 1970s alongside a sister car, the Pontiac Firebird.

1967 Chevrolet Camaro Z-28

Engine 4942cc 90-degree V8

Bore x stroke 101.7 x 76.3mm

Valvegear Pushrod-operated overhead valves

Fuel system Single Holley carburettor

Power 290bhp at 5800rpm

Suspension Front: double wishbones and coil springs; rear: live rear axle with leaf springs and anti-tramp bar

Wheels 15in steel wheels

Brakes Ventilated disc front, drum rear, servo assisted

Top speed 124mph (199km/h)

Below: The Camaro was available in coupé and convertible form, and with a variety of different engines. The RS and SS packages are especially sought-after today.

Dodge Charger Daytona/ Plymouth Superbird

Chrysler's 'B platform' sired the mid-range Dodge Coronet and Plymouth Belvedere saloons, and subsequently the Dodge Charger and Plymouth Road Runner coupés – the latter given a PR boost by a $50,000 deal with Warner Bros to link the car to the cartoon character of the same name (you even got a 'meep-meep' horn).

Both coupés were raced in the American NASCAR stock car racing championship, and in 1969 Dodge developed an aerodynamic package for the Charger which was designed to reduce drag and increase stability on the fast oval tracks, consisting of an 18-inch (46cm) glassfibre nose cone and a 25-inch (63cm) tall rear wing. It was hugely successful – at Daytona that year Dodge finished 1-2-3-4. On the street these wild-looking Charger Daytonas, on sale only in 1969, were available with a choice of two engines, the 440ci (7210cc) V8 with 375bhp or the famous 426ci (6981cc) 'Hemi' with 425bhp.

Plymouth went the same route in 1970, with an aerodynamic kit for the Road Runner: Plymouth called it the Superbird. Again an extended glassfibre nose and tall rear wing were added, though the components were slightly different to those on the Charger Daytona. The engine choice was slightly wider, as the Superbird could be ordered with the 375bhp 440ci V8, the 390bhp 'Six Pack' V8 or the 426ci Hemi with 425bhp. Race ace Richard Petty made it a star of NASCAR.

Just 503 Charger Daytonas were built, and Plymouth sold 1920 Superbirds, but just 70 and 93 respectively were fitted with the Hemi engine. These 163 cars are the crowning achievement of the 'muscle car' phenomenon.

Above: *The massive rear aerofoil helped to keep the tail down at high speed on NASCAR racing versions of the Plymouth Road Runner Superbird, and a glassfibre nosecone reduced drag. Dodge proved the worth of a similar aerodynamic kit on the Charger Daytona the previous year.*

Below: *The bluff front of the Charger R/T received a pointed nosecone on the Charger Daytona, to reduce aerodynamic drag.*

(Ferrari) Dino 206/246GT

Enzo Ferrari's son Alfredo, usually known by the nickname Dino, died young. He was remembered in a line of V6 Ferrari racing machines which began in 1956, all of which carried the name Dino. A V6 road car would follow in the 1960s, marking the debut of the Dino name as a brand for Ferrari's smaller production cars.

The road-going Dino was powered by a new 2.0-litre, 65-degree V6 which Ferrari planned to use in its Formula 2 race cars, which were required to use a production-based engine. The V6 would be built by Fiat, and would later go into high-performance Fiat models.

The basic shape of the road-going Dino was shown by Pininfarina at the Turin show in 1966. It was a supremely lithe and elegant shape, with a characteristic wrap-around rear window and a long rear deck under which the compact V6 engine sat sideways with its gearbox alongside.

The production Dino 206GT (the numbers standing for 2.0-litre, six-cylinder) appeared in 1967, but just 150 were built before the engine was enlarged to 2.4 litres for the 246GT in 1969. The new engine had a wider bore and longer stroke for a displacement of 2418cc, housed in a cast-iron cylinder block with light-alloy heads. Power output climbed to 195bhp at 7600rpm. Other changes to the 246 included steel rather than alloy bodywork with minor dimensional changes, a bigger fuel tank and wider tyres.

The 246GT was replaced by the wedge-shaped, V8-powered Dino 308GT4 in 1973. But the curvaceous 206/246GT endured, and despite being conceived as an 'entry level' car its now one of the most sought-after of Ferraris.

Above and below: *Though never badged as a Ferrari, the Dino is one in all but name. This is a 246GT, the later version with a steel body and a larger, 2.4-litre V6 engine with an iron block.*

Ferrari 365GTB/4 'Daytona'

Above: *The Pininfarina-styled Daytona was the ultimate front-engined Ferrari. In the late 1960s it went head-to-head with its mid-engined rival from Lamborghini, the Miura.*

The dramatic shape of the 365GTB/4, by Pininfarina's Leonardo Fioravanti, made its debut at the Paris show in 1968. After the brutal curves of the outgoing 275GTB/4 the new car showed a beautifully clean and uncluttered line that promised the aerodynamic efficiency vital for a truly impressive top speed.

Providing the power for that high maximum was a new V12 engine derived from the old 250/275 Colombo unit. For the 1963 330GT the V12 had been redesigned with a 71mm bore (all the 250/275 engines were 58.8mm bore) to increase the capacity to 3967cc, and an increase of stroke from 77mm to 81mm enlarged the engine again to 4390cc for the 365 California in 1966. Further fettling boosted the power output to 325bhp at 7500rpm for the 365GTB/4.

The 'Daytona' name was used internally, commemorating Ferrari's 1-2-3 victory in the Daytona 24-hour sports car race in 1967. But, so the story goes, the name was leaked to the press and an incensed Enzo Ferrari instead insisted on using the car's technical nomenclature. But 'Daytona' stuck.

Despite being Ferrari's flagship model, and despite disappointment in some quarters that Ferrari had not yet gone the mid-engined route as Lamborghini already had with the Miura, the Daytona sold well. More than 1400 were built between 1968 and 1974, 123 of them being 365GTS/4 Spyders (convertibles). These open cars are now worth considerably more than standard Daytonas due to their rarity, and incredibly a number of Berlinetta (coupé) cars have been converted into Spyders. In any form, this is the last of Ferrari's great front-engined supercars, and to many eyes the greatest Ferrari of them all.

Ferrari 365GTB/4 'Daytona'

Engine 4390cc 60-degree V12

Bore x stroke 81.0x 71.0mm

Valvegear Twin overhead camshafts per cylinder bank

Fuel system Six Weber carburettors

Power 352bhp at 7500rpm

Suspension Front: double wishbones, coil springs and anti-roll bar; rear: double wishbones and coil springs

Wheels 15in alloy wheels

Brakes Disc brakes all round, servo assisted

Top speed 175mph (282km/h)

Ford Escort Twin Cam/RS1600

Ford's new small car for 1968, the Escort, was an obvious candidate for performance tuning. Following the same recipe that had worked so well with the Lotus-Cortina, the twin-cam Lotus engine was slotted into the engine bay of a heavy-duty Escort bodyshell and the suspension was tweaked to produce the Twin Cam Escort.

It soon became Ford's frontline weapon in rallying, combining the merits of Lotus power with handy size and tidy handling thanks to a well-sorted suspension system with MacPherson struts at the front and a well located live axle at the rear.

To keep the Escort competitive Ford turned to engine specialists Cosworth, who had already produced a Formula 2 engine based on Ford components and had created the DFV F1 engine with Ford money. Cosworth came up with the BDA, with twin belt-driven overhead camshafts operating 16 valves and producing 120bhp. In 1970 the BDA engine went into the Escort RS1600, which kept Ford's name at the forefront of European rallying into the 1970s.

The Twin Cam and RS1600 were the first in a long line of hot Escorts. The 1.6-litre Mexico was named in honour of Ford's triumph in the London-Mexico rally, while the RS2000 offered RS1600-style performance using a 2.0-litre overhead-cam Cortina engine which was cheaper and easier to maintain – though lacked the same tuning potential. The RS line continued with a new range of Escorts in 1975.

Above: *With the Escort Twin Cam and RS1600, Ford created a series of affordable sporting saloons which proved ideal for stage rallying.*

Below: *Ford's win in the London-Mexico rally provided the name for the Escort Mexico, which was fitted with a high-compression 1.6-litre Crossflow engine. It was cheaper than the faster RS1600 and RS2000 models.*

Excalibur

From a casual glance you might think this car belongs in a different chapter, but despite the vintage styling the Excalibur was only conceived in 1964 and its heydey was not in the 1920s, but in the 1970s.

Designer Brooks Stevens created the Excalibur as a show car for Studebaker in 1963, but the company management were worried that this 1920s-style car with heavy overtones of the Mercedes SS would give the public the wrong idea about Studebaker's future models, so they refused to display it. Instead it was presented as a special project by Brooks Stevens Design Associates. It generated so much interest that Stevens' two sons, David and Steve, decided to put the car into production in 1964.

The Studebaker engine was replaced by a 300bhp, 327ci (5359cc) Chevrolet unit, and the body panels changed from aluminium to glassfibre. Early cars were all two-seat roadsters following the original prototype, but in 1966 a four-seat convertible called the Phaeton was added to the range.

A Series II car with a new chassis and larger engine debuted in 1970, and in 1975 Excalibur introduced a Series III car with another new frame and a big-block 7440cc Chevrolet engine. Production peaked at 367 cars in 1979. Though an economic downturn in the 1980s hit Excalibur hard new cars were built into the 1990s and production may one day resume. After all, the Excalibur's extraordinary style will never be out of date.

Above: *Early Excaliburs were two-seat roadsters, but a four-seat Phaeton convertible was made available in 1966. This is a later model.*

Below: *The extraordinary Excalibur looks like a relic from between the wars, but actually dates from 1964. Mercedes SS-inspired styling is by Brooks Stevens.*

Chapter 5

The 1970s

BMW 02 Saloons

During the 1950s BMW's range was split between the big 'Baroque Angel' saloon and the tiny Isetta bubble car, but with nothing in the lucrative mid-range market. By 1959 the once-proud company had run out of money, but fresh capital came from industrialists Harald and Herbert Quandt. They instigated development of a new mid-range four-door car, known as the Neue Klasse or 'New Class', which reached production as the BMW 1500 saloon in 1962.

A sportier two-door version with a 1.6-litre engine appeared in 1966, at first called the 1600-2 and later renamed 1602. Independent suspension – MacPherson struts at the front, coil-sprung semi-trailing arms at the rear – gave it tidy handling for its time, and in twin-carb, 105bhp 1602ti form it was a natural rival to sports saloons from Alfa Romeo and Lancia.

A cabriolet was added to the range in 1967 and the 2.0-litre 2002 followed in 1968, proving its potential by winning the European Touring Car Championship in the hands of Dieter Quester. A twin-carb 2.0-litre 2002ti soon followed.

In 1971 the cabriolet was replaced by a Targa-top car with a fixed roll hoop behind the front seats, and a three-door Touring was introduced. Kugelfischer mechanical fuel injection was also now available on the 2.0-litre engine, delivering a smooth and economical 125bhp in the 2002tii.

The Ultimate '02' was the 2002 Turbo of 1973, building on technology which BMW had used in its racing saloons since 1969. With 170bhp it offered amazing performance, but tricky on/off power delivery. It was unfortunate enough to be launched just as the early 1970s oil crisis hit, and only 1672 were built.

Top and above: *The 2002 Turbo was the ultimate development of BMW's compact saloon series. The turbo engine offered plenty of power but also lots of lag, so it was rapid but tricky to control.*

Below: *The best all-rounder of the 02 series was the 2002tii, with Kugelfischer mechanical fuel injection and 125bhp. The two-door saloon is the most common, but there were related convertibles and a three-door Touring hatchback.*

NSU Ro80

A fascinating might-have-been, the NSU Ro80 was a fast, comfortable and technically advanced saloon hobbled by the epic fuel consumption and unreliability of its twin-rotor Wankel rotary engine.

NSU and Felix Wankel had first worked together when NSU ran into trouble with the rotary valves it used on its two-stroke motorcycle engines. The NSU Wankel Spider of 1964 was the first production car in the world to use Wankel's rotary engine, a single-rotor unit which produced 50bhp from a displacement of just 497cc. The Ro80 engine was twice the size and developed 115bhp, but it proved to be no more reliable than the earlier unit when the Ro80 was unveiled in 1967. Rotor tip sealing was always an issue, with many cars needing replacement engines after just a few thousand miles. The warranty costs that ensued bankrupted NSU, which was taken over by Volkswagen in 1969.

The Ro80's reliability problems overshadowed what was otherwise a very accomplished car. The cleanly styled four-door body was aerodynamically efficient, offered plenty of interior space and good visibility. All-independent suspension, front-wheel drive and a long wheelbase provided an excellent ride and stable cornering, while the ultra-smooth rotary engine and sophisticated transmission (with a torque convertor and a clutch operated by a pressure switch on the gearknob) made for refined progress.

Many were re-engined with Ford V4 or V6 engines, or Mazda rotaries, but with modern technology the NSU rotary can be made reliable. The Ro80, a liability when new, is finally coming good as a classic.

Above and below: *NSU's Ro80 was an advanced saloon that offered excellent road manners, but its unreliable Wankel engine was its downfall. Many owners replaced them with Ford V4s or V6s, and later Mazda rotary engines were used, but today the technology exists to make the Wankel engine a reliable unit.*

BMW E9 Coupés

The 'Neue Klasse' 2000 saloon sired a 2000C/2000CS coupé in 1965, its handsome lines seemingly related to those of the rare Bertone-styled 3200CS of the early 1960s. Six-cylinder coupés with revised four-headlamp styling followed in 1968, offering 170bhp 2.8-litre engines and 130mph (209km/h) performance. The definitive big BMW coupé, known internally as the E9 series, arrived in 1971 with a full 3.0-litre engine (180bhp in the carburettored 3.0CS, 200bhp in the Bosch-injected 3.0CSi), disc brakes all round and suspension revisions to cope with the broad-shouldered performance.

Racing versions run by Alpina and BMW's own works team enjoyed some success in touring car racing, and to make the cars even more competitive BMW introduced a lightweight 3.0CSL in 1972. Weight was saved by fitting an aluminium bonnet, boot-lid and door skins and plastic side windows, deleting the front bumper and stripping out much of the interior trim. The engine was quoted as 3003cc (instead of 2985cc for the 3.0CSi) allowing the race-prepared versions to run engines of up to 3.3 litres.

The CSL represented BMW in a serious battle with Ford's very special RS Capris in European touring car racing. To keep the CSLs competitive an aerodynamic package was introduced in 1973 which added a deep front air dam, fences along the tops of the front wings, a roof spoiler, and a boot-mounted rear aerofoil. It was said to be worth 15 seconds per lap at the long Nürburgring circuit. Genuine road cars with this 'Batmobile' kit are very rare – and very valuable.

1973 BMW 3.0CSL

Engine 3003cc in-line six

Bore x stroke 89.3 x 80.0mm

Valvegear Single overhead camshaft

Fuel system Fuel injection

Power 200bhp at 5500rpm

Suspension Front: MacPherson struts and anti-roll bar; rear: semi-trailing arms, coil springs and anti-roll bar

Wheels 14in alloy wheels

Brakes Disc all round, servo assisted

Top speed 140mph (225km/h)

Below: In 1973 the racing CSLs were given an aerodynamics kit including a deep front air dam and a rear aerofoil. Road cars with the kit are rare and desirable.

Jaguar XJ6/XJ12

Jaguar's complex range of mid-size saloons, along with the vast 420G, were all replaced at one go by the XJ6 of 1968. It would be Jaguar's front-line model for the best part of two decades, and wasn't finally removed from the Jaguar range until 1992.

William Lyons once again demonstrated his mastery of styling by giving the XJ6 saloon a shape which was elegant and modern, while at the same time hinting at the car's power and performance. Somehow it clearly retained Jaguar's essential values but moved the marque into a whole new era.

Under the attractive new skin much of the XJ6's engineering had been seen before. The engines were derivatives of the long-running XK six-cylinder unit which had been around since the 1940s. The familiar 4.2-litre version was joined by a new short-stroke 2.8-litre. For 1972 the six-cylinder power units were joined by the XJ12, fitted with a revised version of the V12 engine first seen in the Series III E-type the previous year.

Series 2 models arrived in 1973, with detail changes including revised interiors and – most noticeably – a higher front bumper to meet new regulations. The range was expanded with a pair of elegant two-door coupé models, the XJ4.2C and XJ5.3C, backed up by a high profile but ultimately unsuccessful campaign in the European Touring Car Championship run by Broadspeed.

The Series III cars of 1979 did no more than freshen up a range which was starting to show its age, but the replacement XJ40 models did not arrive until 1986 and the XJ12 soldiered on until 1992.

Above and below: *The masterly XJ6 was refined, comfortable, fast and supremely well styled. It replaced Jaguar's entire previous range, a massive gamble, but proved to be extremely popular. This is a Series 2 car with the raised bumper line and smaller front grille.*

Morgan Plus 8

Pre-war styling, traditional craftsman construction and modern performance combine in the Morgan Plus 8, providing a unique blend which was a consistent sales success for Morgan for more than a quarter of a century.

Morgan built three-wheelers until 1935 when it moved to four wheels with the 4/4. In the 1950s Morgan introduced the more powerful Plus 4, using Triumph TR four-cylinder engines, but when Triumph adopted a six-cylinder engine for the TR5 Morgan was unable to follow – because the longer engine would not fit into the Morgan engine bay.

Instead Morgan adopted Rover's ex-Buick 3.5-litre all-alloy V8 engine, which provided an unstressed 160bhp. That gave the new Plus 8 acceleration in the E-type class, though the top speed of 125mph (201km/h) reflected the high drag induced by the attractive, but old-fashioned, body shape.

At first the Plus 8 body followed Morgan's usual practice, with an ash frame covered with steel outer panels, but in 1976 a lightweight alloy body was made available as an option. In 1977 the Moss four-speed gearbox was replaced by a Rover unit which offered a more precise gearchange and an extra ratio.

Engine revisions followed in the 1980s, with fuel injection offered as an option and eventually as standard, and a 3.9-litre engine adopted in 1990. Ultimately a 4.6-litre Rover V8 was offered for the top-of-the-range model.

Production of the Plus 8 came to an end in 2004 when a Ford V6 engine replaced the Rover V8 in a model simply called the Roadster.

Above: *Pre-war styling and handling were joined by very modern performance in the Rover V8-engined Morgan Plus 8.*

Below: *The Morgan shape is instantly recognisable. It has remained largely unchanged since the Plus 4 of the 1950s, and is still in production today.*

Reliant Scimitar GTE

Alongside the famous three-wheeler utility vehicles Reliant built a series of sporting cars, beginning with the Sabre in 1961 and the Ogle-styled Scimitar GT coupé in 1965. After Ogle reworked the Scimitar as a novel sporting estate show car for glass manufacturer Triplex, Reliant refined the idea and put the estate GTE into production in 1968. It found a gap in the market hardly anyone had realised existed, and was such a success that Reliant dropped the Scimitar coupé to concentrate on fulfilling GTE orders.

The GTE – known internally as the SE5 model – followed a similar recipe to the GT, with a box-section steel chassis supporting a glassfibre body, with a front-mounted Ford Essex V6 engine. An uprated engine and a revised interior were introduced in the 1971 SE5a.

In 1975 Reliant produced a bigger, softer GTE code-named SE6 – longer, wider and with updated sharp-edged styling. Ford's Cologne V6 engines were adopted for the SE6b of 1980.

Despite the introduction of a GTC convertible (with a T-shaped roll-over bar reminiscent of the Triumph Stag) Reliant struggled in the recession-hit 1980s and production ended in 1986. A rescue by Middlebridge Motors promised much but only a handful more cars were built before that venture failed, too.

Despite the ignominious end the Reliant Scimitars, particularly the GTEs, are fine cars. They are attractive, practical, have an excellent ride/handling compromise and plenty of performance from the no-nonsense Ford power units. They're characterful classics.

Above: *The handsome Scimitar GTE was an innovative blend of Ford V6 power, tidy handling and estate-car space. It created a whole new market sector, which manufacturers such as BMW, Volvo and Lancia were quick to exploit.*

Below: *Ford's tough 3.0-litre V6 'Essex' engine powered the Scimitar GT, and the first incarnation of the GTE. It was mounted well back with the spare wheel in the nose.*

Aston Martin V8

David Brown's long stewardship of Aston Martin came to an end in 1972. The new owners quickly unveiled revised versions of the existing DBS six-cylinder and V8 models, though the six would only ever be built in small numbers. From the early '70s until the end of the '80s, Aston Martin's staple product would be the V8 saloon. At first the troublesome fuel injection system fitted to the DBS was retained, but in 1973 it was replaced by a quartet of downdraught Weber carburettors.

A longer, four-door Lagonda derivative was launched in 1974, but just seven were built. Meanwhile Aston Martin was facing a financial crisis, and was perilously close to oblivion before being rescued by a consortium of businessmen.

In 1977 a high-performance version of the V8 was announced, under the 'Vantage' name long associated with the fastest Astons. Capable of the 0-60mph (97km/h) sprint in 5.2 seconds, it was quite probably the fastest accelerating production car in the world – and certainly the fastest four-seater. The following year a convertible, the V8 Volante, was added to the range.

Fuel injection made a reappearance in 1986, and around the same time a limited-production V8 Vantage Zagato was announced. Soon a new Aston, the Virage, was under development. The final V8s were built in 1989, two decades after the launch of the original DBS V8.

1972 Aston Martin V8

Engine 5340cc 90-degree V8

Bore x stroke 100.0 x 85.0mm

Valvegear Twin overhead camshafts per cylinder bank

Fuel system Fuel injection

Power Not quoted; 300bhp estimated

Suspension Front: double wishbones, coil springs and anti-roll bar; rear: De Dion with trailing arms, Watt link and coil springs

Wheels 15in alloy wheels

Brakes Disc all round, servo assisted

Top speed 155mph (249km/h)

Below: *Twin headlamps replaced the quadruple lamps of the DBS. The V8 continued with only detail changes until 1989.*

Datsun 240Z/260Z

Britain abandoned the Big Healey market, but the gap was quickly filled by Datsun's 240Z. Albrecht Goertz – responsible for the BMW 507 – penned a neatly resolved fastback coupé shape which really caught the imagination of sports car buyers, particularly in the US.

Healey-style broad-shouldered performance came from a 2.4-litre straight-six engine with a single overhead camshaft, fitted with twin Hitachi carburettors and good for 150bhp. All-independent suspension, rack and pinion steering and disc front brakes meant the 240Z easily had the chassis to live up to its performance. Successes in the tough sport of rallying (something the Big Healey had also been noted for) proved the car's speed and toughness.

As exhaust emissions standards tightened the power output dropped, and after four years the 240Z was supplanted by the 2.6-litre 260Z. The extra capacity raised the power output to 162bhp. The new car also had bigger rear lights and a new interior, and for the first time there was the option of a long wheelbase version with two-plus-two seating.

In the US the engine was enlarged again in 1975, to 2753cc, and the car was renamed the 280Z. It was replaced by a much larger, softer and altogether less exciting 280ZX in 1978.

Three decades on the 'Z cars' are rightly renowned for their combination of performance, looks, handling and toughness. Though corrosion can be a serious problem, as with many steel-bodied cars of the era, they're among the more sensible classic sports car choices.

Above and below: *The Goertz-designed Datsun 240Z effectively plugged the gap in the market left by the demise of the Big Healey. The looks were combined with punchy performance provided by a 2.4-litre straight-six engine.*

VW-Porsche 914

Late in the 1960s Volkswagen and Porsche collaborated on a new mid-engined sports car. Volkswagen wanted something to replace the slow-selling VW Karmann Ghia Type 34, while Porsche was looking for an entry-level model to slot in below the 911. The plan was to produce a single bodyshell, which could be equipped with VW or Porsche engines to suit each marque's needs. The result was the 914, launched in 1969.

Two versions were available: the cheaper 914/4 was powered by a 1679cc Volkswagen engine developing 80bhp, while the 914/6 had the 2.0-litre, 110bhp flat-six out of the Porsche 911. The six-cylinder car was only produced until 1972, when it was replaced by a new model with a 2.0-litre version of the VW engine, developing 100bhp.

At Volkswagen's insistence the 914 was marketed in Europe as a VW-Porsche, while in the US it was known only as a Porsche. Despite some concerns about the odd styling – which some claim was by industrial designer Hans Gugelot – the 914 sold well in the US. But in Europe a high price slowed sales.

A further development was the 916 of 1971. By installing the 190bhp, fuel-injected engine from the 911S, Porsche turned the 914 into a 145mph (233km/h) performance car. But production costs would have been too high, and Porsche cancelled the 916 after a few prototypes had been built.

Production of the 914 continued until 1975, when it was replaced by a new joint Volkswagen/Porsche project which had become the Porsche 924.

Above: *Arguments persist as to whether industrial designer Hans Gugelot created the look of the 914, as some have claimed.*

Below: *The mid-engined 914 was initially available with an 80bhp Volkswagen engine or a 110bhp Porsche flat-six. Later the Porsche engine was superseded by a 2.0-litre Volkswagen unit with 100bhp.*

Alfa Romeo Montreal

The Alfa Montreal was first seen at the Expo '67 World Fair in Canada, the car featured a striking Bertone shape with seven horizontal slots behind each door which suggested that the engine might be mid-mounted. But the show car was built on an Alfa Giulia platform and carried its engine in the nose – and the engine was nothing more exciting than a 1.6-litre Alfa twin cam.

Rumours that the Montreal was powered by the V8 engine from Alfa's Tipo 33 race car were wide of the mark, but not for long. The production Montreal which followed three years later was altogether swifter: under the ducted bonnet lay a 2593cc version of the all-alloy racing V8, fed by SPICA fuel injection. It developed 200bhp, detuned from the 440bhp of the 3.0-litre racing engine.

The Montreal's suspension was shared with the contemporary GTV, a competent combination of double wishbones at the front and a well-located, coil-sprung live axle at the rear. With a top speed potential of nearly 140mph (225km/h), serious brakes were a must and the Montreal had four big ventilated discs to haul the speed down.

Though the Montreal looked and sounded fantastic, it never achieved the sales success that it deserved. Just 3925 were made between 1970 and 1977. Sales dwindled after the 1973 oil crisis, when thirsty cars such as the Montreal were looked on as anti-social. Today, though, it makes a fascinating classic.

Top and above: *Alfa Romeo's Montreal was wonderful, if flawed. It was dramatic inside and out, and powered by a detuned race engine developing 200bhp.*

1972 Alfa Romeo Montreal
Engine 2593cc 90-degree V8
Bore x stroke 80.0 x 64.5mm
Valvegear Twin overhead camshafts per cylinder bank
Fuel system Spica fuel injection
Power 200bhp at 6500rpm
Suspension Front: wishbones, coil springs and anti-roll bar; rear: live axle with coil springs, trailing arms and A-bracket
Wheels 14in alloy wheels
Brakes Ventilated disc all round, servo assisted
Top speed 135mph (217km/h)

Citroën SM

Since the mid-1960s Citroën had been keen to add a prestige car to its range, and in 1968 the French firm entered into a partnership with Maserati to supply a suitable engine. Maserati built an all-alloy 2.7-litre V6, unusual for its 90-degree angle between the cylinder banks (which suggests a relationship with Maserati's V8s, though in practice few parts are interchangeable between the two). The engine went into a steel monocoque body with a teardrop taper in plan view that meant the rear track had to be nearly 6in (152mm) narrower than the front.

Naturally the new car, called the SM, used Citroën's hydropneumatic suspension system, made famous by the DS, with interconnection between front and rear on each side and automatic self-levelling. At the back the wheels were suspended from DS-style trailing arms, but the front wheels were mounted on unequal length transverse arms to keep the front wheels vertical as the body rolled, minimising understeer.

As with the DS, the hydraulic system not only maintained the SM's ride height, it also levelled the headlights and steered the inner lamps into corners, and provided power for the brakes and steering. With just two turns between locks the steering was very direct but had no true feedback, so artificial 'feel' was engineered into the system.

Sadly the SM succumbed to a combination of the early-'70s oil crisis and Citroën's mounting financial troubles. Nearly 13,000 were built before production ended in 1975.

Above: *Citroën's flagship GT car, the SM, combined elements of the DS saloon and a Maserati-sourced 2.7-litre V6 engine. The high-geared steering and power brakes take some getting used to, but the SM is a superb touring car.*

Below: *SM could never be mistaken for another car. Like the DS it had a powered hydraulic system which operated the suspension, brakes and steering – it even swivelled the headlamps as the car turned into a bend.*

De Tomaso Pantera

Alejandro de Tomaso's first road car was the 1965 Vallelunga, with a backbone chassis, glassfibre body and mid-mounted 1498cc Ford Cortina engine tuned to produce 102bhp. In 1966 much the same chassis was fitted with a Ford V8 engine and rakish Giugiaro-styled bodywork to produce the Mangusta, with scorching straight-line performance but troublesome handling.

De Tomaso's next project was the Pantera, which left behind the pressed-steel backbone frame of previous cars in favour of a full steel monocoque body structure designed by Giampaolo Dallara, with styling by Tom Tjaarda at Ghia (another company owned by de Tomaso). Again power came from a mid-mounted Ford V8, this time a 5763cc Cleveland unit developing 310bhp, enough to propel the car beyond 150mph (241km/h). From 1973 there was an even more powerful Pantera GTS, with a 350bhp V8.

Cannily, de Tomaso forged links with Ford in the US and the Pantera was made available through Lincoln Mercury dealerships, a massive boost to the car's sales prospects. Sadly the Pantera was hampered by awful build quality which led to rust and unreliability – Elvis Presley shot his when it failed to start – and Ford pulled the plug in 1974. Production continued, though in smaller numbers, while de Tomaso busied himself with takeovers of Maserati, Innocenti and motorcycle manufacturer Moto Guzzi.

The Pantera remained in production throughout the 1980s, growing wide arches and wings in wild GT5S form. It was restyled in 1990 by Marcello Gandini, and was finally replaced by the BMW-engined de Tomaso Guara in 1993.

Above and below: *Italo-American Pantera combined wedge-shaped supercar looks with reliable power from a 5.8-litre Ford V8. Production continued in small numbers right through to 1993.*

Maserati Bora/Merak

The late 1960s saw mid-engined cars complete their takeover of sports car racing, and road car manufacturers such as Lamborghini and Ferrari started to follow suit. Maserati, now owned by Citroën, joined the move to mid-engined supercars in 1971 with the Giugiaro-styled Bora.

The sleek monocoque body concealed new all-independent suspension engineered by Giulio Alfieri and Citroën-style powered hydraulics operating the brakes, adjusting the seats and pedals, and raising the retractable headlamps. Power came from Maserati's 4.7-litre V8 engine, already familiar from the Ghibli, Mexico and Quattroporte, which was mounted longitudinally behind the cabin and drove through a five-speed transaxle. From 1976 the engine was enlarged to 4.9 litres and 335bhp, enough to power the Bora to nearly 170mph (274km/h).

In 1972 Maserati introduced a sister car to the Bora, called the Merak, with much the same structure but with the fastback rear end replaced by a flat rear deck and curious 'flying buttresses'. The Merak was fitted with a smaller V6 engine derived from that in the Citroën SM (usually 3.0 litres but also available as a 2.0-litre in Italy) and the cabin was lengthened so that two extra seats could be squashed into the back.

Early cars had a 190bhp engine but with Ferrari's V8-powered Dino 308GT4 on the way Maserati tuned the V6 to deliver 220bhp for the 1974 Merak SS. The Merak became Maserati's staple model, selling more than 1000 examples before production ended in 1983.

1973 Maserati Bora
Engine 4719cc 90-degree V8
Bore x stroke 93.9 x 85.0mm
Valvegear Twin overhead camshafts per cylinder bank
Fuel system Four Weber carburettors
Power 310bhp at 6000rpm
Suspension Front: wishbones, coil springs and anti-roll bar; rear: wishbones, coil springs and anti-roll bar
Wheels 15in alloy wheels
Brakes Ventilated discs all round with high pressure hydraulic assistance
Top speed 160mph (257km/h)

Below: *Bora supercar was designed by Giugiaro and powered by Maserati's familiar V8 engine, enlarged to 4.9 litres.*

Pontiac Firebird Trans Am

Above: *More than a million Pontiac Firebirds were sold during the 1970s.*

Pontiac's Firebird was the sister car to the Chevrolet Camaro launched in 1967, only minor styling details and trim differentiating the two. When a new Camaro was unveiled for 1971 there was a new Firebird too – and it would rack up more than a million sales during the 1970s.

Fastest of the Firebird range was the Trans Am, which peaked in 1973 with the arrival of the SD-455 engine option. It was listed as a 290bhp engine (to comply with a rule that no General Motors product could have more than 300bhp) but in reality the 455ci V8 was crammed with NASCAR know-how and very little had to be modified to turn it into a 540bhp race motor. It was probably the most powerful engine Pontiac ever offered in a road car.

In the early 1970s the Trans Am was also offered with a 400ci V8 and a regular specification 455ci engine, but gradually the high-performance units were dropped as emissions laws bit ever harder. By 1977 the 400ci engine was the most powerful available, and that year the nose was restyled with four small square headlamps inset into the front panel, instead of the original pair of round lamps. Another restyle in 1979 gave the Firebird an attractive twin nostril front end. In 1980 the standard engine was a 301ci unit, with a turbocharged version as an option and a 305ci Chevy small block as an alternative. A lighter new generation Firebird took over in 1981.

The Trans Am remains most people's idea of an American performance car. Its image was memorably reinforced by its starring role alongside Burt Reynolds in the *Smokey and the Bandit* films.

Below: *Bold graphics were all part of the Trans Am's appeal to American buyers.*

Fiat X1/9

In 1969 the Italian styling house Bertone unveiled a striking Fiat-engined show car which it called Runabout, a wedge-shaped open two-seater sports car with a prominent built-in roll-over hoop. Fiat liked the idea, and it was developed into production form to replace the 850 Spider. Bertone was contracted to build the bodyshells, which were sent to Fiat for final assembly.

The car's development codename, X1/9, was adopted for the production machine. Early cars were powered by the 75bhp, 1.3-litre Fiat 128 engine, mounted behind the front seats and driving the rear wheels. Two luggage areas were provided, one in the nose (shared by the spare wheel) and another behind the engine. With new safety regulations expected to ban full convertibles in the US, the X1/9 was instead provided with a removable 'targa' roof panel.

Offering sharp mid-engined handling, mini-Ferrari looks and a safe and versatile package, the X1/9 was very well received. But it needed more power, and in 1978 it was upgraded with the 1498cc engine from the Ritmo/Strada, coupled to a five-speed gearbox. Even then, there was only 85bhp to play with, and in the US emissions regs resulted in as little as 67bhp.

The car took on a new identity in 1983 when Bertone took over complete assembly, and fitted its own badges. The X1/9 survived until 1988, when production ended with a 'Gran Finale' special edition.

Above: *Bertone came up with the original X1/9 concept, and at first built the bodyshells for Fiat. In 1983 Bertone took over assembly of the car.*

Below: *Mini-Ferrari looks and excellent mid-engined road manners made the X1/9 appealing, even if performance in a straight line was never exceptional.*

TVR 3000M

Martin Lilley's takeover of Blackpool sports car manufacturer TVR in 1965 was accompanied by revisions to the products and the addition of an 'M' to each car's designation.

The home market had two choices of engine, both from Ford: the 1600M was powered by the 1.6-litre 'Crossflow' in-line four from the Ford Escort, while the 3000M used the 3.0-litre 'Essex' V6 from the Capri. The 138bhp 3000M was good for 124mph (199km/h) and could sprint from rest to 60mph (97km/h) in 7.6 seconds.

For the US market, with its tight controls on exhaust emissions, TVR offered a 2500M powered by the 'Federalised' twin carburettor version of Triumph's 2.5-litre straight six – the same 105bhp engine used in the US-market Triumph TR250 and TR6 sports cars.

All the cars were built on a bespoke steel tube chassis with well-sorted double wishbone suspension all round producing excellent handling. The bodywork was all glassfibre, with a characteristic wrap-around rear window.

A rare turbocharged version of the 3000M, developed by Broadspeed, was available from 1975 and the hatchback Taimar was introduced in 1976. In 1978 TVR announced a very handsome cabriolet version, which was to be the last new variant: all the cars were replaced by TVR's new wedge-shape Tasmin in 1980.

But the wedge era proved to be short-lived: late in the 1980s TVR – now headed by Peter Wheeler – reintroduced the 1970s styling on the S series cars, which would outlast the wedges and set up TVR's modern success with the Griffith, Chimaera and Cerbera.

Above: *M-series TVRs marked the arrival of new company owner Martin Lilley. Under the glassfibre body there was an accomplished steel-tube chassis. The 3000M was fitted with a 138bhp Ford V6 engine although a few cars had a Broadspeed turbocharged V6.*

1973 TVR 3000M
Engine 2994cc 60-degree V6
Bore x stroke 93.7 x 72.4mm
Valvegear Pushrod operated overhead valves
Fuel system Single Weber carburettor
Power 138bhp at 5000rpm
Suspension Front: double wishbones, coil springs and anti-roll bar; rear: double wishbones and coil springs
Wheels 14in alloy wheels
Brakes Disc front, drum rear, servo assisted
Top speed 125mph (201km/h)

Ferrari 365/512BB

The letters 'BB' meant Berlinetta Boxer, which denoted a fixed-roof coupé car with a flat or 'boxer' 12-cylinder engine mounted amidships. It was Ferrari's answer to the Lamborghini Miura, and its replacement for the front-engined 365GTB/4 'Daytona'.

That magnificent engine was a 4.4-litre unit (each cylinder displacing about 365cc, giving the car its designation) which had its roots in the 3.0-litre Ferrari Grand Prix engine. In the BB it sat above its gearbox, which meant the centre of gravity was higher than in some competing mid-engined cars using the classic layout with the gearbox at the back of the car in unit with the final drive. As a result the BB's handling was trickier than it might have been, but with 360bhp on tap and a 175mph (282km/h) top speed (early claims of 200mph/322km/h were wide of the mark) few were complaining.

The BB was based on a tubular structure with aluminium and glassfibre panels. Styling, almost inevitably, was by Pininfarina, which made a superb job of blending aggression with poise, elegance and understatement in a crisp modern wedge.

From 1976 the engine was bored and stroked to increase the capacity to 4942cc for the 512BB (the number this time standing for five litres and 12 cylinders). As with other Ferraris, fuel injection was adopted in place of the serried rank of Weber carburettors in the early 1980s.

The BB continued to head Ferrari's line-up until the introduction of the Testarossa, using a development of the same flat-12 engine, in 1985.

Above: *The interior of the Berlinetta Boxer was neat and workmanlike rather than sumptuous, as was traditional Ferrari style. This is the 5.0-litre 512BB version of 1976.*

Below: *The dramatic wedge-shaped nose of the BB normally hid these pop-up headlamp units. The flat-12 engine was mid-mounted with the gearbox underneath.*

Lamborghini Countach

Above: *Upwards-opening doors were a unique feature of the Lamborghini Countach, designed to make entry and exit easier in confined spaces. The Countach was the arch-rival of Ferrari's Berlinetta Boxer in the 1970s.*

The Miura's replacement was just as eyecatching, but it was constructed in a completely different way. Where the Miura structure was built up from folded sheet metal with the engine mounted transversely, the Countach used a multi-tube structure with a longitudinal engine orientation, and the gearbox was mounted ahead of the engine between the seats. The engine itself was essentially the same 4.0-litre V12 that had powered the Miura, with a peak output of 385bhp.

The striking body shape was the work of Marcello Gandini at Bertone, marking the first use of the kinked rear wheel arch shape which Gandini would return to again and again in the future. Dramatic 'butterfly wing' doors opened upwards to make entry and exit easier.

The clean lines of Gandini's shape were interrupted by enlarged air ducts, an optional rear aerofoil, wide wheel-arch extensions and 'telephone dial' alloy wheels on the 1978 LP400S, and in 1982 a bigger 4.7-litre engine was introduced in the LP500S. In 1985 the V12 was enlarged again, to 5.2 litres, and given four valves per cylinder in the Countach QV (the letters standing for 'quattrovalvole' or 'four valve'). Power rose to 455bhp.

The final development of the Countach was the Anniversary model of 1989, which celebrated a quarter of a century of Lamborghini cars. Styling revisions carried out in-house updated the shape, though the result was no more attractive than Gandini's original. The last Countach was built in the summer of 1990: it was replaced by the equally dramatic Diablo.

1977 Lamborghini Countach LP400S

Engine 3929cc 60-degree V12

Bore x stroke 82.0 x 62.0mm

Valvegear Twin overhead camshafts per cylinder bank

Fuel system Six Weber carburettors

Power 375bhp at 8000rpm

Suspension Front: double wishbones, coil springs and anti-roll bar; rear: double wishbones and coil springs

Wheels 15in alloy wheels

Brakes Ventilated discs all round, servo assisted

Top speed 170mph (274km/h)

Lancia Stratos

Above: *Lancia's Stratos was designed specifically as a rally car, with a striking wedge shape, short wheelbase for nimble handling and power from a Ferrari V6 engine.*

Below: *This view of the Stratos emphasises the short wheelbase and wide tracks which made it an ideal rally car. The Stratos won the Monte Carlo Rally for three consecutive years in the 1970s, and two World Makes Championship titles.*

Fiat took a controlling interest in two great Italian makes in 1969. Ferrari and Lancia both came under the control of the Turin-based giant, and that was to make possible one of the most glorious performance cars of the 1970s – the Lancia Stratos.

The idea came from Lancia competitions manager Cesare Fiorio. Inspired by the mid-engined Stratos concept car which Bertone displayed at the Turin Show in 1970, Fiorio suggested building a mid-engined car specifically designed to be a rally winner, powered by the iron-block Ferrari Dino 246GT engine which was soon to become redundant as the 246GT made way for Ferrari's new Dino 308GT4.

The Stratos was given a stiff steel monocoque with unstressed glassfibre outer panels. Wide tracks and a very short wheelbase gave the car high levels of grip with a nervousness to its handling which compromised it as a road car but made it ideal for rallying.

Though the new car made its competition debut in 1972, running in a prototype category, production (at Bertone) did not begin until 1974. Lancia was supposed to build 500 examples to homologate the Stratos into the production car categories, but only 492 were ever completed. Meantime the Stratos racked up numerous rally victories, including consecutive wins in the Monte Carlo Rally in 1975-76-77, and won the World Championship of Makes for Lancia in 1975 and 1976.

Rarity, competition success and that Ferrari engine combine to make the Stratos the ultimate post-war classic Lancia.

Alfa Romeo Alfetta GT/GTV

A new range of Alfa Romeo saloons, the Alfettas, appeared in 1972. They revived the name of a pre-war Grand Prix car, and the use of the name was appropriate because the new saloon echoed the racing Alfetta's use of a De Dion rear suspension system and rear-mounted gearbox. The front suspension was by torsion-sprung wishbones, and power was provided by the familiar 1779cc Alfa twin-cam in-line four.

In 1974 the saloon was joined by a coupé which was similar mechanically but very different visually. In place of the saloon's rather upright styling the coupé was a curvaceous fastback, the original design for which had been created by the prolific Giorgetto Giugiaro. At first the Alfetta GT had a 1.8-litre twin-cam engine like the saloon, but in 1976 that was superseded by a choice of 1.6-litre and 2.0-litre power units with 109bhp and 130bhp respectively. The 2.0-litre car was known as the GTV, where the V stood for Veloce, Italian for speed.

In 1981 Alfa Romeo added a new top-of-the range model to the Alfetta GT range. A magnificent new 2.5-litre V6 engine had been introduced with the (otherwise unloved) Alfa 6 saloon, and a fuel-injected version of that engine was now dropped into the Alfetta coupé shell to produce a model called the GTV6. With 160bhp on tap, the GTV6 could reach 127mph (204km/h) and it had the most exciting engine note this side of a Ferrari.

Above and below: *The Alfetta GT and GTV coupés were based on the mechanicals of the Alfetta saloon, with a rear-mounted gearbox and De Dion rear suspension. All are characterful cars, particularly the swift V6-engined GTV.*

Lotus Esprit

Lotus boss Colin Chapman aimed to move the company upmarket in the 1970s, and the new generation of Lotus cars beginning in 1974 with the Elite which was bigger, faster and flashier than its predecessors. The new Lotus sports car for 1976 was the Esprit, carrying the Elite's 2.0-litre, 16-valve in-line four amidships in a steel backbone chassis which carried striking Giugiaro-designed wedge bodywork. Early publicity came when Roger Moore demonstrated an Esprit's qualities both on the road and underwater in the James Bond film *The Spy Who Loved Me* in 1977.

Regular updates addressed early problems, and in 1980 a much more mature 2.2-litre Esprit was released alongside an exciting new Esprit Turbo (which also became 007 transports, in *For Your Eyes Only*). Turbocharging the engine boosted the power output from 160bhp to 210bhp and turned the Esprit Turbo into a genuine 150mph (241km/h) car. Ferraris were still quicker, but it made the Esprit much more competitive.

The Esprit's sharp 1970s lines became more and more dated, until Peter Stevens softened the edges with a clever restyle in 1988. In 1996 Lotus added its own 3.5-litre, 349bhp V8, which finally gave the Esprit the performance to live up to its looks. Production continued until as late as 2004, and though no direct replacement was announced when Esprit production ended there are persistent rumours that Lotus plans to launch a new Esprit very soon.

1977 Lotus Esprit
Engine 1973cc in-line four
Bore x stroke 95.2 x 62.9mm
Valvegear Twin overhead camshafts, 16 valves
Fuel system Twin Dellorto carburettors
Power 160bhp at 6200rpm
Suspension Front: double wishbones, coil springs and anti-roll bar; rear: transverse links, driveshaft links, semi-trailing arms and coil springs
Wheels 14in alloy wheels
Brakes Discs all round, inboard at rear, servo assisted
Top speed 135mph (217km/h)

Below: *This is an early Esprit, but the profile changed little until Peter Stevens restyled the car in 1988.*

Ferrari 308/328 GTB/GTS

Above: 308GTB was Ferrari's volume model in the 1970s. The neat styling was by Pininfarina.

The mid-range Ferrari from the latter half of the 1970s to the end of the 1980s was this spiritual successor to the much-loved Dino 246GT. Unlike that car the original 308GTB was powered by a V8 engine, a four-cam 3.0-litre unit (308 denotes 3.0 litres and 8 cylinders) developing 255bhp which was carried over from the 308GT4. In Italy, where large-capacity engines were severely taxed, there was also a highly-tuned 2.0-litre 208. The GTB was in effect based on a short wheelbase GT4 chassis, with Pininfarina styled bodywork in a mixture of steel and glassfibre panels until 1977 – thereafter the bodies were all-steel.

In 1978 an open-top GTS was added, much in the mould of the old 246GTS – the roof panel was removable but the rear buttresses remained, so the open-air effect was limited.

Increasingly stringent emissions regulations in the late 1970s started to restrict the power outputs of the later carburettored engines, and a move to fuel injection in 1980 brought an improvement in emissions but limited power still further. Four-valve cylinder heads were developed to boost output, and were fitted to the QV (Quattrovalvole, Italian for four-valve) models in 1983.

In 1985 the 308 was replaced by a 3.2-litre 328, offering more power and more refinement but perhaps lacking the 'edge' of the earliest 308s. The line ended in 1989 when the 348 was announced, but to many Ferrari aficionados the 308/328 is a better bet than its successor.

Below: The 328GTB of 1985 had a larger engine and more power, but it wasn't as sharp on the road or track as the 308.

Ford Escort RS Mk2

When Ford announced a new generation Escort in January 1975 enthusiastic drivers assumed the range would include high performance models to replace the first generation Mexico, RS2000 and RS1600 Escorts. Instead the news was grim: the Advanced Vehicle Operations production line at Aveley in Essex, where the Mk1 RS Escorts were built, was being closed down.

Replacements for the earlier RS Escorts did come, but it was not until 1976 before they arrived – and production of the new cars was entrusted to the main Escort facilities at Halewood in England and Saarlouis in Germany. As before there were three models, each aimed at a slightly different customer.

The 'entry level' car was the Escort RS Mexico, powered by a 1.6-litre Pinto engine with 95bhp (replacing the Mk1 Mexico's 86bhp Crossflow engine). The MacPherson strut front suspension and live rear axle followed standard Escort practice but the spring rates and damping were firmed up to provide wieldy handling at the expense of a jiggly ride.

As before the Mexico was joined by an RS2000 Escort with a 2.0-litre Pinto engine, offering 110bhp and a 110mph (177km/h) top speed. The RS2000 was instantly recognisable by its four-headlamp 'shovel nose'.

Primarily intended for competition use, the RS1800 was the fastest of the three RS Escort models. The big difference was under the bonnet, where the RS1800 had a new version of the Ford Cosworth BDA engine, enlarged to 1835cc and producing 115bhp. It became one of the greatest rally cars of its era, winning the World Championship in 1979.

***Above:** The matt-black rear panel and boot spoiler denote RS Escort, in this case the 2.0-litre Pinto engined RS2000. The RS2000 was designed as a high-performance road car, while the RS1800 had more competition potential.*

***Below:** The glassfibre 'shovel nose' with four headlamps is a characteristic feature of the RS2000 – the only RS Escort to be fitted with it.*

Jeep CJ-7

Above: *Option packages such as the Golden Eagle and this, the Laredo, improved the CJ-7's image and boosted its popularity.*

Willys developed the wartime 'General Purpose' or GP vehicle into the post-war 'Civilian Jeep' or CJ series. The first civilian model available in quantity was the CJ-2A, followed by the CJ-3s of the early 1950s. The longer, wider CJ-5 (based on the military M-38A1 Jeeps used in the Korean war) was introduced in 1954 and would continue in production right through to 1983 with numerous changes and improvements along the way – though the classic Jeep silhouette would remain largely unchanged.

By 1970 the Jeep brand had come under the control of the American Motors Corporation, and AMC six-cylinder and V8 engines were now the usual Jeep power units. In 1976 AMC introduced a new Jeep which was a milestone in the development of the series, the CJ-7 – still retaining the classic Jeep looks and the utilitarian nature, but now offering such refinements as automatic transmission and a removable hard top and steel doors. The CJ-7 also came with Jeep's Quadra-Trac fully-automatic four-wheel-drive system. It was these which helped the CJ-7 to become the fastest-selling Jeep model in the 1970s (though the CJ-5 sold more in total, thanks to a longer production run) as the American public looked for fun, go-anywhere vehicles that were well-equipped and easy to use. Special editions such as the Golden Eagle and Laredo added to the Jeep's image and popularity.

CJ-7 production ended in 1986, when the model was replaced by the Wrangler YJ. Though the Wrangler looked similar to the CJ – apart from its controversial rectangular headlamps – it was a very different machine.

Below: *CJ-7 was the fastest selling Jeep in the 1970s. After the utilitarian nature of early Jeeps, the CJ-7 introduced automatic transmission and Quadra-Trac four-wheel-drive.*

Porsche 911 (930) Turbo

Porsche began developing turbochargers to increase the performance of its petrol engines in 1969. Turbochargers were employed with great success on the fearsome 1000bhp 917-10 and 917-30 cars which won the Can-Am racing series in 1972 and 1973.

In 1974 Porsche raced an experimental turbocharged 911 Carrera, and the debut of a turbo road car came that year at the Paris Salon. The 911 Turbo went into production the following year with Bosch K-Jetronic fuel injection and a KKK turbocharger boosting the 2993cc air-cooled flat-six engine to 260bhp (compared to 230bhp for the most potent normally-aspirated engines) which gave the car a top speed of 160mph (257km/h). A prominent 'whale tail' rear spoiler was fitted to the engine cover to help reduce aerodynamic lift at speed. Though this was Porsche's flagship 911 it didn't have the five-speed gearbox fitted to lesser 911s because the 'box wouldn't stand up to the extra torque of the turbo engine.

In 1978 that engine was bored out to give 3299cc. At the same time an intercooler was added to cool the compressed air being supplied to the engine, thus improving the unit's volumetric efficiency and reducing the risk of pre-ignition. The 3.3-litre Turbo with around 300bhp remained one of the fastest road cars on the planet until the end of production in 1989.

In 1990 a new 964-based Turbo was quickly brought to market, but it retained the old engine with modifications improving power to 320bhp. It was replaced by a turbo version of the latest 3.6-litre engine in 1993.

1979 Porsche 911 (930) Turbo 3.3
Engine 3299cc flat six
Bore x stroke 97.0 x 74.4mm
Valvegear Single overhead camshaft per cylinder bank
Fuel system Bosch fuel injection, KKK turbocharger
Power 300bhp at 5500rpm
Suspension Front: struts, torsion bars and anti-roll bar; rear: semi-trailing arms, torsion bars and anti-roll bar
Wheels 16in alloy wheels
Brakes Ventilated discs all round, servo assisted
Top speed 160mph (257km/h)

Below: *Wide arches covering fat tyres and a 'whale tail' rear spoiler were the most noticeable changes to the classic 911 shape.*

Triumph TR7/8

Few cars represent so plainly the malaise of the state-owned British Leyland combine in the 1970s, hampered by inadequate management and a militant workforce. The TR7 was designed to replace the increasingly old-fashioned separate-chassis TR6 roadster. Taking into account new safety legislation in the US which seemed certain to outlaw open cars, the wedge-shaped car was designed as a fixed-head coupé with styling by Harris Mann. The engineering was deliberately kept simple because American buyers had told Triumph they liked cars that were reliable and easy to fix if they went wrong.

The concept had much to commend it. Though the TR7's single-cam, four-cylinder engine had only 105bhp (even less in emissions-strangled US spec) the chassis could clearly handle more power. To address that Triumph planned to fit the 127bhp 16-valve Dolomite Sprint engine in a 'TR7 Sprint', and a pilot run of prototype cars was built (some of them being used as works rally cars). But a four-month strike at the Speke, Liverpool factory where the TR7 was made caused production to move to Canley, Coventry and ended any chance of production for the 16-valve version. When Canley was closed the TR7 assembly line was moved again, to the Rover plant at nearby Solihull.

A TR8, with the Buick-derived 3.5-litre Rover V8 engine under the bonnet, did reach production and there were drophead versions of both the TR7 and TR8 (when those threatened safety regulations failed to appear). Good though they both were, they were too little, too late, and by 1981 the TR7 was dead – and the mass-market British sports car with it.

Above: *The wedge-shaped TR7 came as a shock to TR diehards. The front-mounted single-cam four developed just 105bhp, but more powerful versions with 16-valve and V8 engines were planned from the start.*

Below: *The V8-powered TR8 answered criticisms of the TR7's performance. The drophead body was much prettier and more versatile than the fixed-head coupé.*

Volkswagen Golf GTI

Originally a spare-time project by a group of Volkswagen engineers, the GTI was adopted by the company as a homologation special for motor sport, to be built in strictly limited numbers. That all changed when the car was put on sale, and VW realised it had an enormous hit on its hands.

The recipe was a simple one already proven by such cars as the Mini-Cooper and Lotus-Cortina: take a good, modern family car, give it a peppery engine and tweak the suspension for optimum handling. Volkswagen started with the compact, lightweight three door Golf, with its attractively crisp 'folded paper' styling by Giorgetto Giugiaro, and added a 1.6-litre four-cylinder engine boosted by Bosch K-jetronic fuel injection to develop 110bhp. Power was sent to the front wheels through a five-speed manual gearbox. Stiffer springs and anti-roll bars at both ends took care of the handling, while disc brakes and a servo made sure the stopping ability was up to the task.

UK buyers had to wait until 1979 for official right-hand-drive versions and only ever got the three-door body – some markets could choose a five-door shell. A 1.8-litre engine was introduced for the final cars built before the Mk2 Golf took over – a more mature but softer and heavier car. The original GTI is an important car: it started the 'hot hatch' phenomenon of the '80s.

Above and below: *Hot hatch fans the world over are grateful to Volkswagen for spotting the potential in a spare-time project that had been undertaken by some of its engineers. There have been five generations of the Golf GTI but the original remains the most admired.*

Porsche 924/944

Above: *Porsche designed the 924 for Volkswagen, but took over the project itself. The 924 would lead to the 944 (with a proper Porsche engine in place of the 924's Volkswagen/ Audi unit) and later the restyled 968.*

Despite the relative lack of success of the 914 joint venture, Porsche and Volkswagen moved on to a new sports car project in the early 1970s. This time the plan was to create a new sports coupé using as many existing VW and Audi parts as possible in order to keep production costs to a minimum. Porsche designed the car, then Volkswagen changed its mind – and instead of letting a good idea go to waste Porsche decided to build the new car itself as an entry-level model.

The Porsche 924, as it was called, broke new ground for Porsche in several areas. It was the company's first front-engined car, the first Porsche with a water-cooled engine (a tough but uninspiring in-line four) and it was to be built in what for Porsche was a new factory – the old NSU/Audi works at Neckarsulm.

The design was neat, if a little anonymous, but now that it was a Porsche rather than a Volkswagen what it lacked was real performance. More power came in 1979 with the launch of a 924 Turbo, followed by the 944 powered by a new 2.5-litre in-line four which was effectively half a 928 V8. In 1985 Porsche introduced a 944 Turbo which combined rapid straight-line pace with modern grip and handling: many said it was more than a match for the fastest 911s in real world driving.

The 944 was heavily revised to become the 968 in 1991, recognisable by its 928-style lamps inset into the nose. Production of the 968 continued until 1995.

1977 Porsche 924
Engine 1984cc in-line four
Bore x stroke 86.5 x 84.4mm
Valvegear Single overhead camshaft
Fuel system Bosch fuel injection
Power 125bhp at 5800rpm
Suspension Front: MacPherson struts and optional anti-roll bar; rear: semi-trailing arms, torsion bars and optional anti-roll bar
Wheels 14in alloy wheels
Brakes Disc front, drum rear, servo assisted
Top speed 120mph (193km/h)

Porsche 928

Dr Ernst Fuhrmann took over as Porsche chief executive in 1971. Fuhrmann believed the 911's days were numbered – it was already eight years old, and the concept of a rear engine and air cooling dated back to the 356 of 1947 – and that Porsche had to press ahead with water-cooled, front engined machinery. At the top of this new range would be the 928.

It was introduced at the Geneva show in 1977. The rounded styling looked alien at the time, but anticipated some of the 'organic' forms which other car manufacturers would begin to use in the 1980s. Under the bonnet was a 4.5-litre water-cooled V8 engine which fed its 240bhp to a rear-mounted gearbox. The front suspension used wishbones and coils, while the rear was an independent layout which Porsche called the 'Weissach axle', after its research and development facility. Unlike the 911, the 928 was available with either manual or automatic gearboxes.

Though fast and well-built the 928 seemed to lack the character of the 911 and certainly failed to take over from the older car as Fuhrmann had wished. In 1979 Porsche introduced a 928S with a bored-out 4.7-litre engine – the first of a series of uprates which gradually made the 928 faster and changed its emphasis from luxury GT car to a more driver-focussed sports coupé. The last of the 928s had 5.4-litre engines and revised styling, and were built in 1995.

Above: *Deformable plastic panels replaced conventional bumpers on the Porsche 928, giving the car a clean and uncluttered appearance.*

Below: *The 928's styling was fresh and dramatic, though the shape had aerodynamic drawbacks (as the spoilers and air dams quickly fitted to revised models proved). It was designed to replace the 911, but failed.*

Saab 99/900 Turbo

The VW Golf GTI had made small sports cars seem outdated and irrelevant in the 1970s, and the Saab Turbo threatened to do the same with many a mid-range performance machine. It was fast, reliable, well-built, practical and with turbocharged power it was enormous fun to drive.

Saab had introduced the 99 in 1967, offering a more modern body shape and greater space than the 96 models. Despite their fine front-drive chassis the most powerful engine offered was the 118bhp fuel-injection unit in the 99EMS – until the advent of the Turbo, first seen at the Frankfurt show in 1977.

Adding a turbocharger to the injected 2.0-litre engine boosted the power output to 145bhp, turning the 99 Turbo into a swift performance machine. Though 99s were available with two, three, four or five doors, early 99 Turbos were all based on the three-door 99 Combi bodyshell. Four-door cars followed and a series of two-door Turbos was built to homologate the model for rallying (replacing the 99EMS). Later there was a short run of five-door Turbos.

In 1978 Saab introduced the 900, following the same lines as the 99 and carrying over the Turbo engine, but with a longer nose and longer wheelbase. In 1984 there followed the 900 Turbo 16, with a 16-valve engine developing 175bhp. A very smooth 'Aero' bodykit was available, which raised the top speed of the 900 to 130mph (209km/h).

Saab continued to build 900s until 1993, when a new generation model based on a European GM platform took over.

Above and below: *Turbo power turned the staid but well-built Saab 99 into an exciting road car. This is the 900, with a similar but larger body. The 16-valve engine introduced in 1984 offered the most power, 175bhp.*

Chapter 6

Modern Classics

Jaguar XJ-S

1975 Jaguar XJ-S
Engine 5343cc 60-degree V12
Bore x stroke 90.0 x 70.0mm
Valvegear Single overhead camshaft per cylinder bank
Fuel system Fuel injection
Power 285bhp at 5750rpm
Suspension Front: wishbones, coil springs and anti-roll bar; rear: transverse links, driveshaft link, twin coil spring/damper units and anti-roll bar
Wheels 15in alloy wheels
Brakes Disc all round, inboard at rear, servo assisted
Top speed 155mph (249km/h)

Jaguar replaced the E-type with the XJ-S, more a refined GT than a true sports car. Much of its engineering was carried over from the successful XJ6 and XJ12 saloons, which meant independent suspension and disc brakes all round, and the remarkable 5.3-litre V12 engine – the only mass-production V12 of the time.

But the styling of the XJ-S drew as many brickbats as plaudits, while the build quality of all Jaguars at that time was poor, and as fuel prices rose the car's epic fuel consumption made it unpopular.

In 1981 Jaguar redeveloped the V12 engine using a new cylinder head design, incorporating the 'Fireball' combustion chamber design invented by Swiss engineer Michael May. The new V12, together with a higher final drive and some cosmetic improvements, went into a 'High Efficiency' XJ-S in 1981. A further fillip came with the introduction of a new cabriolet, powered by a brand new engine – a 3.6-litre straight-six which would also be seen in the new XJ40 saloons.

In the US Bob Tullius' Group 44 team ran a wild spaceframed XJ-S, while in the UK Tom Walkinshaw's TWR team won the European Touring Car Championship in 1984. TWR's expertise hit the road in 1988 with the XJR-S, at first with a 318bhp 6.0-litre V12 and later uprated to 332bhp.

Jaguar introduced a full convertible, smoothed out the coupé's looks and uprated both the mainstream V12 and the six-cylinder as the XJ-S enjoyed a resurgence in popularity. It finally made way for the XK8 in 1996.

***Below:** Though the XJ-S effectively replaced the E-type, it was more of a GT than a sports car. Not everyone praised its looks. The low nose hides either Jaguar's V12 engine or the AJ6 six-cylinder. The XJ-S was turned into a European Touring Car Championship winner by Tom Walkinshaw and TWR.*

Audi quattro

In the mid-1970s Volkswagen designed an off-road 4x4 called the Iltis, largely by plundering the existing Volkswagen/Audi parts bin. Iltis experience led Audi engineers to investigate the benefits of four-wheel-drive in a high performance road car, and that work would lead to a four-wheel-drive road car in 1980 – the Audi quattro.

Power came from a turbocharged version of Audi's in-line five-cylinder engine, already under development for the 200 5T saloon and producing 170bhp. For the quattro it gained an intercooler and an electronic ignition system with an intake air temperature sensor, together with higher boost (up from 0.75bar to 0.85bar, about 12psi) and a bigger exhaust system, boosting the output to 200bhp.

It was an instant sensation, with motoring journalists reaching for their thesauruses to find new superlatives. A revised version arrived in 1984 with wider wheels, stiffer suspension and a controversial talking digital dashboard.

The quattro was an obvious candidate for rallying, and though works quattros made an inauspicious debut in 1981 with accidents and unreliability, they were soon winning. To make the car still more competitive Audi created a shorter-wheelbase Sport quattro with an alloy 20-valve engine developing 304bhp.

In 1988 the standard quattro was revised with a 2226cc engine and Bosch engine management system, while the transmission now incorporated a self locking Torsen centre differential. In 1990 a 20-valve head was introduced, raising the quattro's power to 220bhp. By 1992 the aerodynamically shaped S2 quattro had taken over, but legions of quattro fans still maintained the original was the best.

Above: *The flat-faced wheelarch extensions were characteristic of the quattro. Four-wheel-drive traction and roadholding were remarkable.*

Below: *The boxy quattro body hid 2.2 litres of turbo power, four-wheel-drive and anti-lock brakes.*

BMW M1

Interest in top-level sports car racing declined in the 1970s, and there were calls for a more 'relevant' formula with more of a link to production cars. The Group 5 'Silhouette Formula' was the result – racing machines based on production cars, with significant technical modifications allowed provided that the race cars still looked similar to the road cars from the side, and kept major components such as the engine in the same location.

The BMW Turbo concept car of 1972 provided the basis for a limited-production supercar, the M1, from which competitions manager Jochen Neerpasch could develop the racer. The body shape was refined by ItalDesign, while the 2002 Turbo engine was replaced by a 24-valve straight six developed from those already used in BMW's CSL coupé racing programme. In 1976 Lamborghini was engaged to turn the basic idea into a workable road car and then build the 400 units required for homologation, but Lamborghini was in financial trouble and by the end of 1977 it still had not completed the job. Exasperated, BMW turned to German coachbuilder Baur to build the M1 production cars.

After all that, the 'Silhouette' formula never really caught on. Instead BMW created a new racing series, Procar, supporting eight rounds of the F1 World Championship. All the cars were M1s, and the drivers included some Grand Prix stars though contractual conflicts meant many F1 men did not take part. Procar ran for just two seasons, Niki Lauda emerging as 1979 champion and Nelson Piquet winning in 1980. Just 455 M1 road cars were built, the last of them in 1981.

Above: *ItalDesign was responsible for the final BMW M1 shape. The car was powered by a mid-mounted, 24-valve straight six developing 277bhp in road form.*

Below: *BMW's traditional 'kidney' grille was echoed in the M1's intakes. Racing M1s sprouted wide arches to cover huge wheels and fat slick tyres, but the road car was more restrained.*

Chevrolet Corvette

GM's fourth-generation Corvette for 1984 improved on the old car's aerodynamics, reduced its weight and improved its crash performance. As if that wasn't enough, in time the new Corvette would bring new levels of performance and the return of a popular bodystyle.

The 1984 Corvettes were stiffer and safer than before. Weight was cut using composite leaf springs in the rear suspension, aluminium brake calipers and lighter discs. A low-built wedge shape with a penetrating nose and raked-back windscreen helped improve the Corvette's aerodynamics, aiding both its top speed and its fuel economy in a cruise. Though power outputs remained low – just 205bhp from a 350ci (5735cc) V8 – enthusiastic drivers could at least order a manual gearbox, with overdrive as an option.

At first all these Corvettes were coupés with lift-off roof panels, but for 1986 GM reintroduced the Corvette convertible. Anti-lock braking also became available, and new fuel injection boosted the V8 engine to 230bhp.

Drivers looking for more power had two options. Chevrolet's own Corvette ZR-1 was powered by the LT-5 engine, a four-cam 350ci V8 with four valves per cylinder which was developed in the UK by Lotus Engineering, then another part of the General Motors empire. The LT-5 produced 375bhp, which was delivered via a 6-speed manual gearbox. As an alternative, tuner Reeves Calloway produced 500 twin-turbo Corvettes, said to be capable of 200mph (322km/h). The fifth generation Corvette, offering even more power and still greater aerodynamic refinement, took over in 1997.

Top and above: *The new body for the 1984 Corvette made significant improvements to the vehicle's aerodynamics. The coupé with lift-off roof panels was joined by a full convertible in 1986.*

1990 Chevrolet Corvette ZR-1
Engine 5732cc 90-degree V8
Bore x stroke 99.0 x 93.0mm
Valvegear Twin overhead camshafts per cylinder bank, 32 valves
Fuel system Fuel injection/engine management
Power 375bhp at 6000rpm
Suspension Front: double wishbones, transverse leaf spring and anti-roll bar; rear: double wishbones, transverse leaf spring and anti-roll bar
Wheels 17in alloy wheels
Brakes Disc all round, anti-lock system
Top speed 175mph (282km/h)

Toyota MR2

Toyota began work on a small mid-engined sports car in the mid-1970s, no doubt with one eye on the success of the Fiat X1/9 and another on the increasing lack of competitiveness from British marques such as MG and Triumph. But serious development work did not begin until 1980, the result being the MR2 of 1984.

It was a compact and purposeful two-seater with a fixed roof, and a fashionable wedge shape with pop-up headlamps. There was a choice of two engines, a 1.5-litre unit with just 83bhp and a much more exciting (and far more common) twin-cam 1.6-litre with 122bhp. That made the MR2 a brisk performer, well up to the standards of its class – but its trump card was its handling and roadholding, which few rivals came close to matching.

In 1986 Toyota introduced a 'T-bar' roof option, which had twin removable roof panels which could be stowed away to provide a taste of open-top motoring. The stout roll hoop remained fixed in place to maximise crash protection and also body stiffness ensuring that the handling and roadholding qualities were retained. The fixed-roof MR2 was still available, but the T-bar proved to be a popular option.

A more powerful supercharged MR2 was available in some markets, though not in the UK. It offered an extra 22bhp and improved torque throughout the rev range making it much quicker in a straight line.

The MR2 was replaced by a larger Mk2 model in 1989. To many enthusiasts the new car lacked the character and the drivability of the original – and Mk1 MR2s are increasingly sought-after.

Above: *The twin-cam, 16-valve engine with 122bhp was the more exciting of the two power units available in the MR2 – some markets could also buy an 83bhp 1.5-litre version.*

Below: *An MR2 with everything open. The engine was mid-mounted, with luggage space available at the extreme tail end and in the nose. As well as being exciting to drive, the MR2 was a reasonably practical sporty car.*

Mercedes-Benz 190E 2.3-16

New for 1983 was the 190, a compact saloon from Mercedes-Benz. At first just two models were available, both fitted with 2.0-litre engines and differentiated by the use of carburettors (on the 90bhp 190) and fuel injection (on the 122bhp 190E). In the Autumn of 1983 two additional 190s were introduced, a 190D diesel and a high performance version called the 190E 2.3-16.

The designation indicated that the new car was powered by a 2.3-litre engine with 16 valves. The new engine, which had been developed in Britain by Cosworth, was based on the four-cylinder M102 unit familiar from the larger 230E saloon, but the freer breathing cylinder head helped to boost the power output from 136bhp to 185bhp.

By the time the 190E 2.3-16 made its public debut at the Frankfurt show late in 1983 it had already proved its potential at the Nardo test track in Southern Italy, where three prototypes had set long-distance world records for 25,000km, 25,000 miles and 50,000km with an average speed of almost 250km/h. The model would become the basis for Mercedes-Benz entries in touring car racing.

In 1988 a heavily revised 190 was introduced, and the top model was upgraded with a 2.5-litre, 195bhp engine to become the 2.5-16. At Geneva in 1989 an Evolution version was presented, with modifications to improve tuning potential and larger aerodynamic devices. That year 502 were built, all of them painted blue-black metallic. An Evolution II with 235bhp followed in 1990, and again 502 blue-black examples were made. The regular 190E 2.5-16 continued until 1993.

Above and below: *Mercedes' entries in touring car racing were based on the 190E 2.3-16 and 2.5-16, with engines developed by Cosworth.*

BMW M5

1995 BMW M5 3.8
Engine 3795cc in-line six
Bore x stroke 94.6 x 90mm
Valvegear Twin overhead camshafts, 24 valves
Fuel system Fuel injection/engine management
Power 340bhp at 6900rpm
Suspension Front: MacPherson struts; rear: semi-trailing arms and coil springs
Wheels 18in alloy wheels
Brakes Ventilated discs all round, anti-lock system
Top speed 155mph (249km/h)

BMW introduced a heavily revised version of its mid-range 5 Series saloon in 1981, known internally as the E28. In 1984 it added a new performance model to the range, powered by a 218bhp version of the familiar 3.5-litre 'big six'. It was available in two versions, the 535i and M535i, both of which were handsome saloons with 140mph (225km/h) potential. The only difference between them was the presence of sill extensions and a badging on the M-series car.

The M1 supercar had been given a 24-valve, 277bhp version of the in-line six, and after minor revisions (boosting power to 286bhp) that engine went into the 6 Series coupé to produce the M635CSi, an instant Porsche 928 rival. The 24-valve engine also went into the 5 Series shell, creating a new performance saloon which BMW simply called the M5.

Thanks to the saloon bodyshell's lighter weight, the M5 was even faster than the M635CSi, and its conservative appearance meant the performance it offered was all the more surprising. It could easily exceed 150mph (241km/h), yet it was refined, docile in traffic, and had sure-footed handling. The M5 was spacious, practical and luxurious yet it had awesome performance figures, and it made cramped and unreliable supercars seem irrelevant.

From then on every succeeding generation of the 5 Series has been topped by an M5, beginning with the E34 model in 1988, adopting a V8 engine in the 1998 E39 and a 507bhp V10 in the latest E60.

Below left: *The M5 was the ultimate Q-car, with unexceptional looks and four-seater space, but shattering performance.*

Below and bottom: *The six-cylinder 286bhp motor was derived from the M1 and the CSL racing programme. The clinical dash layout favoured the driver.*

Ford Sierra Cosworth

Like the Volkswagen Golf GTI and the Mini Cooper before it, the Sierra Cosworth was intended to be a limited-production homologation special – but it proved to be far more successful than anyone had dared to hope.

Racing engine manufacturer Cosworth conceived a twin-cam conversion for the long-running Ford Pinto 2.0-litre engine, and with the addition of a turbocharger it produced a solid 204bhp, with the potential for much more in racing trim. The engine – Cosworth called it the YB series – was dropped into a three-door Sierra bodyshell, which was given a deep front air dam and a dramatic tailgate-mounted aerofoil. Lowered suspension, wide alloy wheels and fat tyres provided high levels of grip, while inside the road cars were given excellent Recaro front seats and luxurious trim.

Ford built 5500 RS Cosworths at Genk in Belgium, and 500 of those were then reworked as RS500 models with even larger aerodynamic devices, a bigger turbo and still greater tuning potential. The road cars developed 224bhp, while race-spec cars had in excess of 500bhp. The RS500 proved to be almost unbeatable in touring car racing.

In 1988 Ford introduced a subtler Cosworth based on the four-door Sierra Sapphire body, and in 1990 this was given four-wheel-drive and became the basis for Ford's World Championship rally cars. Much the same mechanicals later went into the Escort RS Cosworth.

All the Sierra Cosworths provided scorching performance at a bargain-basement price, and they became an almost automatic choice for anyone who needed a practical and affordable performance saloon. And they're genuine classics.

Above: *A vast rear wing was the three-door Sierra Cosworth's most controversial feature. It became a familiar sight at the front of the grids in touring car racing in the 1980s.*

Below: *The Cosworth-developed engine was a twin-cam four-cylinder unit with a single turbocharger, originally developing 204bhp.*

Ferrari F40

Ferrari celebrated 40 years as a manufacturer in 1987 by building its fastest road car ever, the F40. It was designed to recall the great days of the 1950s and 1960s when sports cars were driven to the tracks where they were raced, but using the best of modern technology and with very modern performance. It would also be the last Ferrari road car to be launched before the death of the company's founder, Enzo Ferrari, in August 1988.

The F40 was based on the 288GTO of 1984, itself a development of the 308/328GTB series. Central to the new car was an enlarged and further developed version of the GTO's engine – a 2936cc V8 with twin camshafts on each cylinder bank, twin IHI turbochargers and intercoolers, and an output of 478bhp. In excess of 600bhp was available in competition tune. The engine was mounted longitudinally in a tubular spaceframe chassis clothed with high-tech carbon fibre and Kevlar composite panels, which helped keep the F40's overall weight down to 1100kg. The aggressive shape, inevitably styled by Pininfarina, was carefully developed to minimise aerodynamic drag and maximise stability – essential in a car which tests proved was capable of 201mph (323km/h), making it for a while the fastest car in production.

Originally Ferrari intended to build just 450 F40s but demand was such that more than 1300 were made between 1988 and 1992 – despite a price tag which would have bought a Testarossa and a 348, and a Lancia Delta to go shopping in!

1987 Ferrari F40
Engine 2936cc 90-degree V8
Bore x stroke 82.0 x 69.5mm
Valvegear Twin overhead camshafts per cylinder bank, 48 valves
Fuel system Fuel injection, twin IHI turbochargers
Power 478bhp at 7000rpm
Suspension Front: double wishbones and coil springs; rear: double wishbones and coil springs
Wheels 17in alloy wheels
Brakes Ventilated disc all round
Top speed 201mph (323km/h)

Below: *The Pininfarina-styled F40 hid its origins well – it was descended from the 308/328GTB series. The new body used Kevlar and carbon fibre composites to reduce weight. Twin turbochargers boosted the F40's 3.0-litre engine to 478bhp, enough for a top speed in excess of 200mph (322km/h).*

Porsche 959

Though Porsche unveiled a Group B racing prototype based on the 911 at the Frankfurt Motor Show in 1983, the first of the 200 production versions required to homologate the car for competition would not reach its owner until 1987. But it was worth waiting for: the 959, as Porsche called it, was a technical triumph and, for a while, the fastest production car in the world.

The 450bhp output necessary to propel the 959 to 197mph (317km/h) came from a new twin-turbocharged version of Porsche's famous flat-six engine. Originally it had been air cooled, but for the 959 Porsche employed its racing experience with water cooling for the cylinder heads. As ever, it was mounted at the rear and delivered power to a complex, computer-controlled four-wheel-drive system. Sophisticated anti-lock brakes and suspension with automatically adjusting ride height (the 959 'sat down' at high speeds to reduce aerodynamic drag) were also part of the formidable technical specification. It was all contained within a 911-derived monocoque body with extended wheelarches and sills, and an integral rear wing.

Prototype 959s used their power and traction to good effect in the tough Paris Dakar rally, winning the event in 1984 and again in 1986. Porsche also entered a 959-based car, the type 961, at Le Mans in 1986. It finished seventh overall and won its class.

Production of the 959 continued beyond the required 200 due to considerable demand. Eventually 250 were built, all left-hand drive, the last of them in 1988.

Top and above: *The twin-turbocharged version of Porsche's flat-six engine powered the 959 to 197mph (317km/h). At the time it was the world's fastest production car.*

Below: *Computer controlled four-wheel-drive ensured that the 959 was never short of traction.*

Mazda MX-5

The affordable front engine, rear-wheel drive open roadster was reinvented by Mazda in 1989 with the MX-5 Miata, in an era when other manufacturers concentrated on fixed-roof coupés and hot hatchbacks. The inspiration for the Mazda was clear: in its basic layout and its looks it had a lot in common with the Lotus Elan of the 1960s. Created with the American market in mind, it was largely developed by Mazda's Californian development centre.

A stiff all-steel monocoque, all-round independent suspension and rack-and-pinion steering gave the MX-5 excellent roadholding and wonderfully controllable handling, making it terrific fun to drive on a twisty road. All-out straight-line pace wasn't the MX-5's forte, though the 1.6-litre twin-cam four that was mounted longitudinally in the nose developed 116bhp and gave the roadster a reasonable turn of speed.

A quicker 1.8-litre version with 140bhp was introduced in 1994, and in 1998 both engines were available in a restyled MX-5 with exposed teardrop-shaped headlamps replacing the original car's pop-up lamps. Subtler tweaks for 2001 sharpened the MX 5's looks a little, and at the same time the 1.8-litre engine was given a new variable valve timing system which increased its output to 156bhp.

A variety of special edition models were produced in the final few years before a new generation MX-5 took over in 2005.

Above: *The MX-5 rejuvenated the small sports car market almost by itself. Performance wasn't exceptional, but it was huge fun to drive.*

Below: *MX-5 styling had echoes of the 1960s Lotus Elan. Later cars had exposed headlamps and larger engines with more power.*

Aston Martin Virage/Vantage

Replacing the long-running Aston Martin V8 saloon was no easy task. A major part of the job was to revamp the Tadek Marek-designed V8 engine, but by the 1980s Aston Martin's engineering resources were slim, and the company called in Connecticut-based Reeves Calloway to update the 5340cc unit with four-valve cylinder heads and maintenance-free hydraulic tappets.

The car that the new engine would power was designed by John Heffernan and Ken Greenley, and was at once elegant and aggressive. The chassis which underpinned it was based on that of the wedge-shaped Lagonda saloon. The new car was christened Virage, and unveiled at the Birmingham International Motor Show in October 1988.

With 335bhp available the Virage could comfortably exceed 150mph (241km/h) and dispatch the 0-60mph (97km/h) sprint in less than seven seconds, but for some Aston customers that wasn't enough. Aston Martin's Works Service division developed an answer, a 6.3-litre engine conversion which boosted power to 465bhp. But even that wasn't enough for some…

At the 1992 Motor Show Aston Martin unveiled the Vantage, a thoroughly reworked and uprated Virage. John Heffernan had revised the styling, giving the Vantage a more aggressive appearance and improving the body's aerodynamic performance. Under the bonnet was a twin-supercharged version of the V8 engine, delivering 550bhp. But some customers wanted still more, and in 1998 Works Service developed a 600bhp conversion which gave the big Aston a top speed in excess of 200mph (322km/h).

Above: *The Virage was the new Aston for the 1990s, boasting a redeveloped version of the Aston V8 engine with multi-valve heads.*

Below: *John Heffernan and Ken Greenley styled the Virage, giving it modern lines, yet with an identifiably Aston flavour.*

Lamborghini Diablo

1990 Lamborghini Diablo
Engine 5707cc 60-degree V12
Bore x stroke 87.0 x 80.0mm
Valvegear Twin overhead camshafts per cylinder bank, 48 valves
Fuel System fuel injection
Power 492bhp at 7000rpm
Suspension Front: double wishbones, coil springs and anti-roll bar; rear: double wishbones, coil springs and anti-roll bar
Wheels 17in alloy wheels
Brakes Ventilated disc all round
Top speed 203mph (327km/h)

The early 1990s saw a whole gaggle of new contenders for the title of world's fastest production car, and for a while in 1991 the fastest of all was Lamborghini's new 202mph (325km/h) supercar, the Diablo.

The model made its debut in 1990 but production cars only began to emerge from Lamborghini's Sant'Agata factory in 1991. Much of the new car's mechanicals were shared with its predecessor, the Countach, but the now-venerable Lamborghini V12 engine was enlarged to 5.7 litres and was good for 485bhp. As before the engine was longitudinally mounted behind the cabin in a tubular spaceframe chassis, which was clothed in aluminium alloy panels. The Diablo, like the Countach, was styled by Marcello Gandini, though it was a more sophisticated and perhaps a less dramatic shape than the outlandish Lamborghinis of the 1970s.

In 1993 Lamborghini introduced the four-wheel-drive Diablo VT, followed up in 1994 by the 525bhp Special Edition. The lightweight Diablo SV and a long-awaited convertible arrived in 1996.

Volkswagen took control of Lamborghini in 1998, and while work began on a Diablo replacement, further developments of the existing car were released. The Diablo GT of 2000 introduced carbon fibre bodywork which helped to reduce weight and at the same time improved build quality. In 2001 the engine was revised and enlarged to 5992cc and the power output climbed to 585bhp. But 2001 was the final year for the Diablo, replaced that year by the first Volkswagen-developed Lamborghini – the Murcielago.

Below: *Like its predecessor the Countach, the Diablo was styled by Marcello Gandini. There's still a hint of the Countach-style distorted rear wheel arch shape. The familiar Lamborghini V12 engine, now in 5.7-litre form, propelled the Diablo into the distance with its 485bhp output. Later cars were even quicker.*

GMC Syclone/Typhoon

Above: *The Syclone pickup was based on the GMC Sonoma, but was fitted with a turbocharged 4.3-litre Vortec V6 engine developing 280bhp. Full-time four-wheel-drive provided traction good enough to allow a 0-60mph (97km/h) sprint time of less than five seconds. The Syclone was followed by the Typhoon SUV, using the same engine but based on the GMC Jimmy.*

With the body of a pickup truck and the acceleration of a supercar, the rare GMC Syclone is one of the more remarkable products of the US motor industry in the 1990s.

Based on the GMC Sonoma pickup, the Syclone derived its extraordinary performance from the sort of engine more likely to be found under the bonnet of a muscle car. The 4.3-litre Vortec V6 was boosted by a Mitsubishi turbocharger, and officially the power output was quoted as 280bhp – but as with all turbo engines, the right weather conditions could drive the power output still higher, and stock Syclones could often exceed 300bhp. To ensure consistent traction whatever the weather or road conditions, the power was delivered to four-speed automatic transmission and a permanent four-wheel-drive system controlled by a central viscous coupling.

The combination of power and traction could propel the big pickup from rest to 60mph (97km/h) in less than five seconds and through the quarter mile in about 14 seconds – though the top speed was limited, by the high and wide pickup shape, to just 125mph (201km/h).

Around 3000 Syclones were built at Production Automotive Services of Troy, Michigan, in 1991. Just a handful more were completed in 1992. That year GMC moved on to the Typhoon, based on the GMC Jimmy SUV and powered by the Syclone turbo V8. Just under 5000 were built in 1992-93. With that the 'SyTy' series ended, sales having been slower than expected. But these are interesting and rare vehicles which might one day be highly prized.

Jaguar XJ220

Above: *Jaguar's XJ220 was originally shown in four-wheel-drive, V12-engined form, but it changed significantly before production began.*

Led by engineering director Jim Randle, a small group of Jaguar engineers developed the first version of the XJ220 supercar in their spare time. It was first seen in public at the Birmingham International Motor Show in 1988, where the curvaceous shape by Jaguar stylist Keith Helfet (also responsible for the beautiful but ill-fated F-type) grabbed as many headlines as the XJ220's ambitious technical specification. It was powered by a multi-valve version of Jaguar's big V12 engine, mid-mounted and driving all four wheels.

But the XJ220 that would go into production in 1992 was a very different car. Behind the scenes TWR, who had operated Jaguar's successful works racing team, had been given the task of building it at a new factory in Bloxham, near Oxford. That job turned into a comprehensive re-engineering of the whole car: out went the V12 engine and four-wheel-drive, and in came a twin-turbo V6 (which TWR had developed for the XJR racing machines) driving the rear wheels. Not that the change left the XJ220 wanting for power: the V6 developed 524bhp, enough to take the XJ220 to a top speed of 213mph (343km/h). That made it the fastest production car in the world.

But some customers were less than happy. The XJ220 had risen significantly in price and had changed considerably since many of them had put down their deposits, and so had the world: economic crises in the early 1990s curtailed the activities of many car collectors, some of whom were speculators who expected to sell at a premium. Just 275 out of a planned 350 XJ220s were built, the last of them in 1994.

Below: *TWR re-engineered the XJ220 using a twin-turbo V6 engine. With 524bhp and a top speed of 213mph (343km/h) it was for a time the fastest production car in the world.*

Dodge Viper

In the 1960s Carroll Shelby was responsible for the Cobra, and late in the 1980s he was back with the Viper – a big two-seat sports car powered by an 8.0-litre Chrysler V10 engine. Such was the reception for this back-to-basics bruiser that development of a production version began early in 1989. The Viper RT/10 went on sale early in 1992.

By then the engine had been reworked by Lamborghini, at the time owned by Chrysler. The original iron-block V10 was designed for use in Chrysler trucks and SUVs, but for the Viper it was redeveloped with an aluminium block, new valve gear (but still pushrod valve operation) and revised combustion chambers which together improved its output to 400bhp. The engine was front-mounted in a tubular steel frame carrying glassfibre panels, and drove the rear wheels through a six-speed manual gearbox.

The result of this work was an extremely rapid car, despite its considerable size and weight. While tipping the scales at no less than 3280lb (1488kg) the Viper had a top speed of 165mph (265km/h) and a 0-60mph (97km/h) sprint time comfortably under five seconds.

A GTS coupé concept was unveiled at the Los Angeles show in 1993, and that entered production in 1996. Better aerodynamics thanks to the fixed roof, and a more powerful 450bhp engine which it also shared with a revised RT/10 roadster, pushed the top speed of the GTS up to 170mph (274km/h). A racing GTS-R version won its class at Le Mans each year from 1998 to 2000, and won the FIA GT2 championship five years out of six.

Top and above: *The Viper sports car and this, the GTS roadster, were big and brutish machines powered by a 5.0-litre V10 engine developed by the then Chrysler-owned Lamborghini. The GTS coupé spawned a GTS-R racing version which was a regular Le Mans class winner and FIA GT2 champion.*

1989 Dodge Viper

Engine 7994cc 90-degree V10

Bore x stroke 101.6 x 98.6mm

Valvegear Pushrod operated overhead valve

Fuel system Fuel injection

Power 400bhp at 4600rpm

Suspension Front: double wishbones, coil springs and anti-roll bar; rear: double wishbones, coil springs and anti-roll bar

Wheels 18in alloy wheels

Brakes Ventilated discs all round

Top speed 160mph (257km/h)

TVR Griffith/Chimaera/Cerbera

Two disparate model lines took TVR into the 1990s. The first was the Ford V6-powered S series, visually related to the TVRs of the 1970s but mechanically much improved. The other was the 420SE, last in a line of wedge-shaped cars which had begun in the 1980s, and were now powered by Rover V8 engines.

The latest S3 chassis and 3.9-litre Rover V8 came together in the Griffith, with a new glassfibre body styled by a team including TVR boss Peter Wheeler. It was in this form that the car was unveiled in 1990, but by the time it entered production a new chassis developed from TVR's Tuscan race car had been adopted, and there was now the option of a 4.0-litre or 4.3-litre V8.

In 1993 a 5.0-litre version of the Rover V8 was introduced in the 340bhp Griffith 500, and TVR introduced the Chimaera – a slightly softer, more practical machine with equally eye-catching glassfibre bodywork.

The Chimaera provided the basis for the two-plus-two Cerbera coupé first seen in 1993. The Cerbera went into production with TVR's new Al Melling-designed 4.2-litre V8 engine, giving it a top speed of 185mph (298km/h) and 0-60mph (97km/h) acceleration in just four seconds. From 1998 that engine was available in 4.5-litre, 420bhp form. From 2000 TVR's latest Speed Six engine was also offered, turning the Cerbera into a characterful grand tourer.

All three of these cars helped to establish TVR as a real player in the European sports car market – and they're distinctive and effective machines.

Above: *The Chimaera blended superb lines and V8 performance with a dose of practicality.*

Below left: *The Griffith marked the emergence of TVR as a serious player. The chassis was related to that of the Tuscan race car.*

Below: *The Cerbera was offered with TVR's own Al Melling-designed 4.2-litre and 4.5-litre V8s, and the related 4.0-litre Speed Six unit.*

Aston Martin DB7

Above: The DB7's beautiful shape was the work of TWR's chief designer, Ian Callum. This is one of the first DB7 press cars.

Ford acquired Aston Martin in 1987, and Jaguar in 1989. It took the combined efforts of all three companies – and a trusted supplier, Tom Walkinshaw's TWR group – to produce a new Aston Martin model which would return the marque to its glory days of the 1960s.

Based on a TWR proposal which had been rejected by Jaguar, the DB7 was built around Jaguar XJ-S running gear and powered by a 335bhp supercharged version of the Jaguar AJ6 straight-six engine. It was launched at the Geneva show in 1993 and production began at TWR's factory at Bloxham, near Oxford, the following year. A Volante drophead followed in 1996.

In 1999 the DB7 Vantage and Vantage Volante were announced. The Jaguar-based straight six engine was replaced by a brand new V12, loosely derived from two Ford Mondeo/Taurus Duratec V6s laid end to end. This 5.9-litre, 420bhp engine gave the DB7 Vantage a top speed of 185mph (298km/h) and a 0-60mph sprint time of 5.0 seconds. The six-cylinder DB7 remained on sale, but very quickly the V12 car took over the bulk of production.

Aston Martin and Zagato rekindled their long-standing partnership in 2002 by producing the 435bhp DB7 Zagato (a lighter, two-seat coupé) and the DB American Roadster 1 (an open-roof California car). The final DB7 variant was the GT, a 435bhp DB7 with aerodynamic tweaks and considerable detail work on the suspension. Production of the DB7 ended in 2003 after just over 7000 had been built, making it by some margin the most popular Aston Martin ever made.

Below: Traditional wood and leather dominated the DB7 cabin, as was expected of an Aston.

McLaren F1

For more than a decade the McLaren F1 was the fastest production car the world had ever seen, the ultimate supercar designed without compromise for optimum speed and driver involvement.

The first discussions about the new car took place in Milan in 1988, where McLaren's Ron Dennis, Creighton Brown and Gordon Murray, and TAG's Mansour Ojjeh waited for a plane. They had just seen McLaren Formula 1 driver Ayrton Senna retire from the Italian Grand Prix after tangling with a back marker, handing victory to Gerhard Berger's Ferrari. Ironically it would be the only Grand Prix that year that McLaren would lose.

The F1 was designed from the ground up with no concessions to development or manufacturing costs. The car's structure was a Formula 1-style tub bonded together from carbon fibre composite mouldings and aluminium honeycomb panels. Three seats were provided with the driver in the centre and located slightly ahead of the passengers, giving him excellent vision and much of the driving sensation of a single-seater race car.

And the McLaren had performance to worry many a single-seater race car, too. It was powered by a 6.1-litre V12 engine developed by BMW, with twin overhead camshafts on each bank of cylinders operating four valves in each combustion chamber and variable inlet valve timing. Maximum output was no less than 627bhp. Despite the electronic wizardry appearing in many other performance cars the McLaren deliberately did without such driver aids as power steering,

Below: *A McLaren F1 on display alongside its 6.1-litre BMW V12 engine, which produced 627bhp in initial form.*

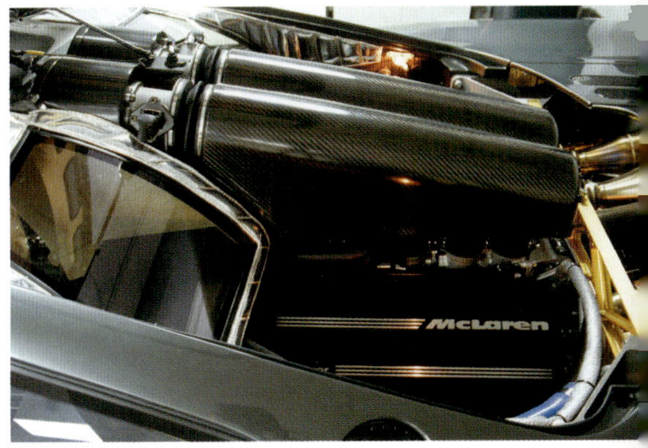

Above: The third F1 prototype, XP3, being demonstrated by former Grand Prix driver Jonathan Palmer.

Top right: The McLaren F1 shattered the record for the fastest production car, being clocked at 241mph (388km/h).

Above: The air intake for the BMW V12 is above the cabin, splitting the rear window in two. The F1's driver was given two interior rear view mirrors to cope with the 'spine'.

semi-automatic transmission or traction control. The braking system had massive cross-drilled steel discs but no anti-lock system. It was all part of designer Gordon Murray's aim to keep weight and complication to a minimum which he felt would maximise driver appeal.

The first prototype, coded XP1, ran for the first time on 23 December 1992 – but it lasted barely three months before it was destroyed in a testing accident. XP2 was completed a couple of days later and took over as BMW's test car. It, too, was crashed – but this time into a concrete block at UK test centre MIRA to prove its safety. Such was the car's strength that it could have been driven back from the crash test, and it was subsequently repaired and used for further testing. Three further prototypes were built before production began, the first customer car being completed in December 1993.

Though the F1 had never been designed as a competition car, new sports car racing rules made it a potential winner and a GTR racing version was developed in 1994. It won at Le Mans in 1995, and won the FIA GT championship in 1995 and 1996. To celebrate, McLaren built a special bright orange F1 LM, with even less weight and even more power. In 1997 three long-tailed road cars were built to homologate a similarly-bodied racer, but with stiffer competition to face the racer could only manage fourth at Le Mans.

Fewer than 100 F1s were built by the time production ended in 1997. Even though the likes of Koenigsegg and Bugatti have built faster cars since, for many the F1 remains the ultimate supercar.

1994 McLaren F1	
Engine	6064cc 60-degree V12
Bore x stroke	86 x 87mm
Valvegear	Twin overhead camshafts per cylinder bank, variable inlet valve timing
Fuel system	Electronic fuel injection
Power	627bhp at 7400rpm
Suspension	Front: double wishbones, hydraulic dampers and anti-roll bar; rear: double wishbones, hydraulic dampers
Wheels	9 x 17in magnesium alloy front wheels, 11.5 x 17in magnesium alloy rear wheels
Brakes	Hydraulic disc brakes all round
Top speed	241mph (388km/h)

Lotus Elise/Exige

Lotus returned to its core values with the Elise – a no-nonsense sports car which derived its performance and road manners from its low weight, and its low weight from innovative structural engineering. Like many previous Lotuses the body was glassfibre but underneath that body the chassis was a completely new concept, a bonded structure largely made from aluminium extrusions. Further weight was saved by the adoption of metal matrix composite (MMC) brake discs, and by the fitment of one of the lightest engines available, Rover's 118bhp, 1.8-litre K-series.

It was quickly clear that the Elise's excellent chassis was crying out for more power, and to address that Lotus announced a 135bhp upgrade package in 1998, and the 143bhp 111S the following year. Later in 1999 the Elise spawned a wild road/track car, the 340R, which was intended to be a modern interpretation of the classic Lotus 7.

In 2000 Lotus unveiled the hard-top Exige (available with 170bhp and 190bhp engine options) and later that year introduced the Series 2 Elise which shared many improvements developed for the Lotus-built Opel Speedster/Vauxhall VX220.

A major change came in 2004 when Lotus adopted the Toyota 2ZZ-GE engine, an all aluminium 1.8-litre twin-cam unit designed by Yamaha. Power jumped to 189bhp and the 0-60mph (97km/h) sprint time dropped below five seconds – but even more importantly for Lotus, this new Elise was developed alongside a 'federal' version which could be sold in the USA. Lotus continues to develop the Elise family, introducing a 218bhp supercharged Exige S early in 2006.

Top and above: *The Elise was, and remains, a lightweight sports car with minimalist interior. Light weight is the key to its rapid performance and excellent road manners.*

Below: *The Series 2 Elise of 2000 offered new, more aggressive styling, and would see the debut of a new engine – a 1.8-litre twin-cam unit from Toyota developing 189bhp.*

Jaguar XK8/XKR

After more than 20 years in production, the Jaguar XJ-S made way for the XK8, in 1996. The new car carried over much of the chassis engineering of the old, but was given a new V8 engine and a stylish new body created under the direction of Jaguar's chief designer, Geoff Lawson.

The new engine, built at Ford's Bridgend engine plant in Wales, was a wonderfully smooth and torque-rich 4.0-litre V8 with twin overhead camshafts per cylinder bank. It was refined and powerful, with a maximum output of 290bhp, and drove the rear wheels through a five-speed automatic gearbox. The subtle combination of the silky engine and almost imperceptible gearchanges made the XK8 a very refined grand tourer – but still with the kind of pace that a dyed in the wool Jaguar buyer expected.

Those who expected even more did not have too long to wait. At the Geneva show in 1998 Jaguar unveiled a new performance version of the XK8, known as the XKR. The V8 engine's capacity was unchanged at 3996cc, but the XKR was fitted with an Eaton M112 supercharger which used a pair of intermeshing helical gears as a pump to cram air into the engine under pressure. The result was an increase in power from the 290bhp of the normally-aspirated XK8 to no less than 370bhp. Though the top speed was artificially limited to 155mph (249km/h), the 0-60mph (97km/h) sprint time of just 5.2 seconds showed the XKR's potential. But there were few external clues to its performance, just a mesh front grille and bigger alloy wheels.

Above: *The supercharged XKR could chase supercars hard, yet offered comfort, refinement and practicality. It was based on the normally-aspirated XK8 of 1996.*

Below: *The XK8 replaced the ageing XJ-S in 1996. Although the new car shared some engineering with the old one, the excellent 4.0-litre V8 engine was all new.*

Ford GT

Le Mans triumphs in the 1960s ensured the GT40 was the ultimate Ford performance car, revered the world over as a classic example of power, looks and achievement. In 2002 Ford decided to recreate that blend with a new car which copied the looks and the basic layout of the GT40 – and it says much about the impact of the original car that it still created so many headlines four decades later.

Called simply the Ford GT, the new car was unveiled as a concept at the North American International Motor Show and just a few weeks later Ford confirmed it would be going into production.

The new car may have looks similar to the old, but it is considerably bigger – 4in (100mm) taller and no less than 18in (457mm) longer – and it is constructed in a different way. The GT's chassis is a modern aluminium structure fabricated from extrusions, castings and stampings. Where the 1960s racer had glassfibre body panels, those of the new GT are super-plastic formed aluminium. Unequal-length double wishbone suspension is used at all four corners, as are four-piston aluminium brake calipers from Brembo, vast BBS alloy wheels and Goodyear Eagle F1 tyres.

Power comes from the biggest of Ford's modular V8s, a 5.4-litre unit with twin overhead camshafts on each cylinder bank operating four valves per cylinder, and a single Eaton screw-type supercharger. The GT has no less than 550bhp at its disposal, enough to propel it to 205mph (330km/h).

2003 Ford GT

Engine 5409cc 90-degree Ford V8

Bore x stroke 90.2 x 105.8mm

Valvegear Double overhead camshafts per cylinder bank

Fuel system Electronically controlled fuel injection, Eaton supercharger

Power 550bhp at 6500rpm

Suspension Front: double wishbones, coil springs and anti-roll bar; rear: double wishbones, coil springs and anti-roll bar

Wheels 9 x 18in front, 11.5 x 19in rear alloy wheels

Brakes Disc brakes all round, servo assisted

Top speed 205mph (330km/h)

Above and below: *Although the GT shares the looks of the 1960s GT40, it is a taller and longer car, and the bodywork is aluminium rather than glassfibre. The Ford GT cabin offers the benefits of modern materials and conveniences.*

Ferrari Enzo

Ferrari's fastest-ever road car was a mid-engined, 660bhp hypercar with innovative braking and electronics systems, named in honour of company founder Enzo Ferrari.

The featherweight chassis, made from carbon fibre and aluminium honeycomb, weighed just 92kg and was clothed in composite body panels, carefully shaped for optimum aerodynamic performance. Ground effects were utilised to create downforce, keeping the car pressed down onto the road at high speed without the need for a large inverted wing at the back of the vehicle.

Power came from an ultra-light 6.0-litre V12 boasting variable inlet and exhaust valve timing and a drive-by-wire throttle, coupled to a six-speed gearbox with electro-hydraulic change operated by paddles behind the steering wheel.

Electronic control systems for the engine, gearbox, suspension, anti-lock brakes, traction control and aerodynamics constantly shared information. For track use the driver could select a more aggressive operation mode which cut gearchange times to just 150 milliseconds and also changed the point at which the traction control system intervened.

F1-style carbon-ceramic disc brakes were fitted, a first for a road car. As well as improving stopping power, they were lighter than steel discs and were designed to last for the lifetime of the car.

Ferrari built 349 Enzos. In 2005 it announced the Fxx, an Enzo-based track car with revised high-downforce bodywork and a 6262cc V12 engine developing no less than 800bhp. The Enzo also formed the basis of the Maserati MC12.

Above and below: *The Enzo is Ferrari's fastest road car so far. The nose deliberately imitates Formula 1 styling, and the Enzo offers plenty of engineering features usually found in F1 racing cars – such as an electro-hydraulic gearchange and carbon ceramic disc brakes.*

Index